SECRET
BALTIMORE

A Guide to the Weird, Wonderful, and Obscure

Evan Balkan

Library of Congress Control Number: 2020938246
ISBN: 9781681060682

Design by Jill Halpin

All photos courtesy of the author unless otherwise noted.

Printed in the United States of America
20 21 22 23 24 5 4 3 2 1

To Molly and Amelia—
our "citying" to take pictures in the early days of
shelter-in-place were the most fun one can reasonably
have during a pandemic.

CONTENTS

INTRODUCTION

In some respects, this was an easy book to write. Easy because Baltimore is loaded with innumerable treasures—many of them hidden—so there was much to choose from. But that, perversely, also made it difficult. When I began this project, 84 entries seemed daunting. When I hit 84 and still had more than a dozen in mind, it became increasingly difficult to exclude some and keep others. Ultimately, in keeping with the thrust of this book, I tried to focus on those items that I thought even longtime Baltimore residents might be surprised by. I also tried to include as many entries as possible that had no associated cost so as to be as accessible as possible. Likewise, I limited myself to sites within the city limits. The official city boundary lines are, in some respects, arbitrary, what with the economic, social, and cultural relationships between Baltimore City and the surrounding counties. But these lines proved useful in managing the large number of entries that ultimately made the cut.

Baltimore is an incredibly varied city, offering up every conceivable lifestyle, supported by the quirky, live-and-let-live attitude typical of port cities. Live Baltimore features more than 250 distinct Baltimore neighborhoods on its website. I've done my best to honor this diversity in the entries I've chosen to include in this book—ethnic, geographic, socioeconomic, etc. (under "Where" in each entry's inset box, the address is followed by the neighborhood name). To that end, visiting all of the hidden treasures listed in *Secret Baltimore* will lead a person literally all across Charm City and guarantee interactions that cut a wide cultural swath. In so doing, the hope is that such visits will reveal how wonderful, vibrant, and energetic our home city really is.

THE AFRO AND THE UPTON

What makes *The Afro-American* newspaper so special?

After the promises of Reconstruction faded into a fierce racial backlash, many African Americans fled the South during the Great Migration, hoping to obtain security in the North. A growing middle class gave rise to a series of newspapers aimed at Black audiences—the *Chicago Defender* perhaps most prominent among them. These publications filled a yawning gap in news coverage as major American newspapers rarely concerned themselves with the lives of African Americans apart from breathlessly reporting "Black crimes"—real and imagined.

The *Baltimore Afro-American*, established in 1892, was one such newspaper. While the vast majority of these papers have disappeared over the years, *The Baltimore Afro-American*, or *The Afro*, as it's known locally, is still going strong, which makes it the nation's longest-running African American family-owned newspaper.

In February 2020, *The Afro* was tapped to occupy the 1838 Upton Mansion after a restoration of more than $7 million. *The Afro* headquarters will move from its offices in Halethorpe once restoration on the Upton Mansion—believed to be the last remaining Greek Revival country house in Baltimore—is completed. Stay tuned.

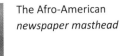

THE AFRO-AMERICAN NEWSPAPER

WHAT: The country's longest-running family-owned African American newspaper

WHERE: 1531 Edgewood St., Halethorpe (after 2021: Upton Mansion, 811 W. Lanvale St., Upton)

COST: None

PRO TIP: Visit online and pick up a subscription: www.afro.com.

That family is the Murphy family, and back in the 19th century, the creator of the paper was John H. Murphy Jr., an extraordinary man who was born into slavery and served in the Civil War with a US Colored Regiment. The paper grew at an astonishing rate thereafter; according to *The Afro's* own historical account, "at one time there were as many as 13 editions circulated across the country . . . [and] During World War II, *The Afro-American* stationed several of its reporters in Europe, the Aleutians, Africa, Japan, and other parts of the South Pacific, and provided its readers with first hand coverage of the war." Many notables wrote for or were otherwise associated with *The Afro*, including Langston Hughes, Sam Lacy, and the artist Romare Bearden, who worked as a cartoonist.

In a digital world in which newspapers face increasing pressure and are folding at an alarming rate, *The Afro* continues, doing what it has always done.

AL CAPONE'S CHERRY TREES

Where will you find cherry trees planted by Al Capone?

America's most famous gangster, Al Capone, lived his final years in the most unpleasant of circumstances: long stints in prison and fighting dementia caused by syphilis. In 1939, recently released from Alcatraz, Capone made his way to Baltimore for medical treatment, intending to go to Johns Hopkins. But officials there, fully aware of Capone's reputation, denied him admittance. So he ended up at Union Memorial, about four miles north, where Hopkins doctors with admitting privileges could attend him.

Hopkins officials made the right call; once installed at Union Memorial, Capone took over an entire floor and installed bodyguards and, terrified of being poisoned, food tasters. He stayed for five weeks and then recuperated in a private home in Pimlico. But as a show of appreciation to Union Memorial, the only hospital that would take him, Capone donated two weeping cherry trees. One was removed during a hospital

Capone cherry tree outside Union Memorial Hospital

expansion in the 1950s. But the other remains to this day, albeit split in half by a 2010 snowstorm. The felled wood was turned into a series of new objects, such as bowls and wine stoppers, and sold at auction as part of a hospital fundraiser.

But in the spirit of a gift that keeps on giving, multiple cherry trees—dubbed "Caponettes" and each a descendant of the original two—are showcased around the hospital campus.

Capone had been to Baltimore before, working as a bookkeeper in the 1920s for the Aiello family in the rowhouse that is today the wonderful Dipasquale's Market in Highlandtown.

ARABBER STABLES

A-what?

It's just about impossible to see animals used as workers in a major city and remain indifferent. It's such an incongruous sight nowadays. The races at Pimlico aside, the sight of horses plodding down Baltimore streets, leading a cart laden with fresh fruits and vegetables, is likely to transport the viewer straight to the 18th century—understandably. After all, the tradition of receiving your edibles via horse cart got its beginning back then.

Sympathize then with a 21st-century denizen, especially a visitor to Charm City, gawking at the sight, as Baltimore remains the only US city that continues this tradition, known locally as "arabbing" (pronounced: Ā-rab-ing). You can go weeks without seeing one and then, out of nowhere, here comes a craftily decorated cart and its equine beast of burden in jangling bells, a human in the lead yelling about his wares and advertising what's for sale. Yes, it might seem a complete anachronism. However, with plenty of food deserts still in the city, making it difficult if not impossible for some residents to get access to fresh fruits and vegetables, the arabbers take on a role beyond mere decorative or nostalgic throwback.

Only a few stalls remain in the city and a small coterie of arabbers who tend to their horses and carts. But if you wish to get a good sense of how this old tradition operates today and

---

Arabbers develop their own distinctive patois, calling out their wares in sing-songy cadences, a style of sale familiar to many travelers and natives in swaths of Latin America and Africa.

*Arabber. Photo courtesy of
Kevin Griffin Moreno*

somehow manages to hang on, a good place to start is the Arabber Preservation Society on Fremont Avenue. It's also an ideal place to get some terrific fruit.

ARABBER PRESERVATION SOCIETY AND STALLS

WHAT: Horse-and-cart produce vendors

WHERE: Locations vary. Preservation Society: 1102 N. Fremont Ave., Upton

COST: Free

PRO TIP: The 2004 documentary, *We Are Arabbers,* can be viewed online at www.folkstreams.net/ film-detail.php?id=256.

THE OTHER ARBORETUM

There's a third arboretum in Baltimore?

Most Baltimoreans know Cylburn Arboretum, that north-central treasure of a place tucked between Northern Parkway, I-83, Coldspring Lane, and Greenspring Avenue. Likewise, the Rawlings Conservancy in Druid Hill is another well-known sanctuary. They are located near one another and also near yet another oasis—albeit smaller and not nearly as well known: Mount Washington Arboretum.

This little gem is merely an acre in size, but it exudes peacefulness and thrives on the love and energy of its volunteers. Mount Washington Preservation Trust began the arboretum in 1999 and has maintained it ever since as a showcase for native plants. Over the years, the trust has added a pond with a waterfall, benches, pergolas, interpretive signs, and a wonderful and inviting entrance archway decorated with tiles

MOUNT WASHINGTON ARBORETUM

WHAT: Another city refuge

WHERE: Tanbark Dr. at Lochlea and Kelly Ave., Mount Washington

COST: Free

PRO TIP: There used to be an apartment complex at this site, but Hurricane David flooded it in 1979, and it was subsequently condemned and torn down. Two decades later, the spot was transformed into this beautiful little garden in this beloved neighborhood.

Take note of the LOVE mural on the concrete retaining wall above the water at the far end of the arboretum. It is one of 20 identical LOVE murals spread across Baltimore City.

Plantings in Mount Washington Arboretum

created by children from Mount Washington Elementary School across the street.

While anyone is free to wander and lose themselves in this wonderful place, the arboretum continues to serve as a center for neighborhood gatherings, hosting solstice parties, Halloween celebrations, outdoor movies, and even weddings.

ARCHAEOLOGICAL MUSEUM

There's another museum at Hopkins?

The Johns Hopkins University campus is host to an internationally renowned art museum, the Baltimore Museum of Art, along with the 1801 Homewood House. But there is another, lesser-known museum (even to many Hopkins students) on campus as well, housed inside the lovely Gilman Hall, whose distinctive bell tower graces many official Hopkins images.

On the lower level of the hall is the JHU Archaeological Museum, which, according to the museum's website, contains "nearly 700 archaeological objects from ancient Greece, Rome, Egypt, the Near East, and the ancient Americas, all exhibited in the custom-built museum facility set within the spectacular Gilman atrium." It's a delight, and a bit of a revelation for many first-time visitors, to come by and peruse the artifacts. But the collection isn't simply for viewing. Befitting Hopkins's esteemed position as the country's first

---

Another free Hopkins offering: in the Steven Muller Building on campus is the JHU Space Telescope Science Institute (STScI), which hosts "colloquia, conferences, lectures, meetings, symposia, and workshops that cover a broad array of topics of interest to the astronomical community as well as the general public." For a list of upcoming events, check stsci.edu/events.

Egyptian sculpture

Johns Hopkins Archaeological Museum collections

JOHNS HOPKINS ARCHAEOLOGICAL MUSEUM

WHAT: A little-known gem of a museum on the Johns Hopkins campus

WHERE: 150 Gilman Hall, 3400 N. Charles St., Johns Hopkins University, Homewood

COST: Free

PRO TIP: Open Monday through Friday, 10:30 a.m. to 1:30 p.m. during academic semesters, plus the first Saturday of each month from 12 p.m. to 4 p.m. Tours can be arranged by appointment.

graduate research institution, the museum also houses "numerous study/display drawers which hold objects such as cuneiform tablets and texts, Egyptian shabtis, ancient and Islamic glass, Hellenistic lamps and Roman stamped bricks . . ."

The pieces in the glass displays can be viewed any time the building is open, making it a wonderful place to stop by almost any time and gain the perspective afforded by many centuries' worth of art and objects.

11

BABE'S BAPTISM

Where was Babe Ruth baptized?

The building that once housed St. Peter the Apostle Church, long referred to as "The Mother Church of West Baltimore," has been looming over the corner of Hollins and South Poppleton since 1842. Back then, the surrounding neighborhood was home to large numbers of Irish immigrants, lured by employment at the nearby Baltimore & Ohio railroad. It's an impressive building, large and brick and fronted by six imposing stone columns.

Declining numbers of parishioners and demographic changes precipitated the church's sale in 2013, and today it functions as the Carter Memorial Church of God in Christ. But when St. Peter the Apostle was still providing services for the Catholic community—about 50 years after its dedication—there occurred an auspicious baptism, though no unique thing

ST. PETER THE APOSTLE CHURCH

WHAT: Where Babe Ruth was baptized

WHERE: Northwest corner of Hollins and S. Poppleton St., Union Square

COST: Free

PRO TIP: St. Peter the Apostle functioned for more than 170 years and was, for that time, the city's second-oldest Catholic church.

Ruth allegedly took a second baptism a little more than a decade later at St. Mary's Industrial School, most likely because his original baptismal certification wasn't available.

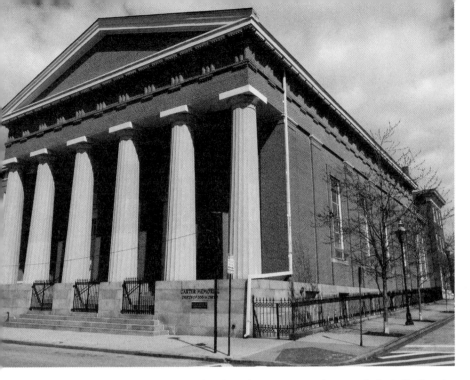

Currently, Carter Memorial Church and once St. Peter the Apostle Catholic Church, where Babe Ruth was baptized

in and of itself. Indeed, it's doubtful anyone could have known on the day of the little one's christening that the baby would ultimately cast one of the longest shadows of the 20th century. The babe being baptized that day would eventually come to be known as The Babe, the greatest baseball player of all time.

George Herman Ruth was born on February 7, 1895, across town on Emory Street. It was three weeks later that he was baptized at St. Peter the Apostle, kicking off a lifelong and somewhat complicated relationship with his Catholic faith. Ruth lived a prodigiously and famously impious life, but he also routinely committed acts of great charity, a practice he ascribed to his religious faith tradition.

BALTIMORE, FRANCE

Where do you find the world's largest collection of Matisse?

I've been to several Baltimores around the world: the subject of this book, of course; the namesake one in Ireland; a nondescript town in Ohio; and even a diminutive collection of huts in the Peruvian Amazon near the Bolivian border (yeah, seriously). But as far I know, there is no Baltimore, France.

Nevertheless, it is not at all surprising that Baltimore's art museums contain works by French masters. But it comes as something of a shock to learn that the world's largest collection of works by one of the most well known of those masters resides right here in this Baltimore.

Along with Claude Monet, Paul Cézanne, Paul Gauguin, and Edgar Degas, to name just a few, Henri Matisse is often cited as one of the towering figures of French art and one of the leading artists of the post-Impressionist, modernist school. Thanks to a 1929 bequest from Claribel and Etta Cone, the Baltimore Museum of Art gained more than 500 pieces created by the artist, including the world-renowned paintings *Blue Nude* (1907) and *Large Reclining Nude* (1935). The acquisition of another 700 or so pieces since then has given the BMA the bragging rights to the largest collection of works by Matisse in the world.

In the BMA's English Sporting Art collection is the Woodlawn Vase, annually presented to the winner of the Preakness Stakes (and then taken back to the BMA), the second of horse racing's Triple Crown. Estimated at around $4 million, it's considered the most valuable trophy in the world of sports.

Baltimore Museum of Art

Baltimore Museum of Art sculpture garden

BALTIMORE MUSEUM OF ART

WHAT: A Matisse treasure trove

WHERE: 10 Art Museum Dr., Johns Hopkins-Homewood

COST: Admittance to the BMA is free, which includes the Matisse works, but there is a charge for special exhibitions.

PRO TIP: You don't even have to step inside to enjoy the art at the BMA. The sculpture garden, to the right of the entrance, is a wonderful place to spend an hour or so. It, too, is free.

And that claim was enhanced by the 2019 announcement of a $5 million gift to establish the Ruth R. Marder Center for Matisse Studies. The 3,500-square-foot facility, slated to open in 2021, will draw visitors and scholars alike, cementing the BMA's earned reputation as a little slice of France on the Patapsco.

BALTIMORE GREENWAY TRAILS NETWORK

Thirty-five miles of green, inside the city?

In 1902, Baltimore's Municipal Art Society commissioned the famed landscape architects, the Olmsted Brothers firm, to design a plan for the city's municipal park system. Published two years later, the plan called for the linking of the city's major green spaces such as Druid Hill, Gwynns Falls, Wyman, and Swann Parks with tree-lined boulevards, the idea being that the natural corridors would encompass important cultural and recreational sites.

The basic notion—spawned from the 19th/early 20th century ideal of providing city dwellers with the opportunity to commune with nature—made Baltimore a city to be envied and emulated in its cultivation and ongoing preservation of its parks. This idea is the continuing inspiration for the Baltimore Greenway Trails Network which,

If you're up for it, you can keep going beyond the city where the Baltimore segment links with the East Coast Greenway, which runs for 3,000 miles from Maine to Florida.

Gwynns Falls Trail

when complete, will stretch 35 miles and run through more than 50 Baltimore neighborhoods.

As of 2020, 25 miles of the trail are already in place. Completion of the final 10 miles will result in a loop with these compass points: Cylburn Arboretum in the north, Cherry Hill Park in the south, Leakin Park in the west, and Herring Run Park in the east.

Of course, even before it's done, hikers, bikers, and walkers can access the trail network at any number of entrances and can more or less choose a distance and go. Ultimately, the 35-mile trail will offer outdoors enthusiasts a panoramic view of Charm City as its character runs the gamut from intensely forested to densely urban terrain. It's a great way to experience all aspects of the city.

TOTALLY BAZAAR

Where can you channel the wonders of the old American Dime Museum?

If you never visited the defunct American Dome Museum, you missed a real Baltimore treat. Its complete weirdness garnered TV spots and write-ups in regional, national, and even international periodicals. The museum showcased an array of bizarre attractions that made the rounds of circus shows and various other old-time curiosity exhibitions. Most of the pieces were real (human hair jewelry, paintings executed by a chimpanzee), but just as attractive were the "authentic fakes," most notably the alleged "Last Turd" of Abraham Lincoln, said to have been retrieved from a Ford's Theater chamber pot (later analysis revealed it included, among other things, Necco wafers) and the severed tongue discovered stuck to a frozen fire plug. And, of course, there was the wonderful Peruvian Amazon giant mummy.

While many still lament the passing of that wonderful old museum, there is an opportunity to get a weirdness fix by visiting Bazaar, "a gift shop specializing in natural history items, home decor, jewelry, and other unique and morbid gifts." It is a place of business, so come with an idea to take something home with you. But browsing isn't discouraged, and those who work there seem to be of perpetually good cheer and ready to answer questions. And inevitably, people have questions—for

---

While the store is full of taxidermy animals, they will not stuff your deceased pet (apparently, people ask for this all the time).

Bazaar store and "Stay Humble, Baltimore" mural

example, "What are the origin stories behind some of the more bizarre offerings, such as the mummified unicorn fetus, the diaphanous rat pup, and the antique embalming hand pump syringe?"

Just like the old Dime, it's often difficult to tell what's "real" and what's not. And that's half the fun.

CURIOSITY SHOP

WHAT: All manner of oddities, for sale

WHERE: 3534 Chestnut Ave., Hampden

COST: Free to visit. Prices for items vary, from a few bucks (vegan fetus) to more than $1,000 (authentic antique human skull).

PRO TIP: Every few months, Bazaar hosts a demonstration by a professional taxidermist. You can sign up for a lesson.

BENNETT BLAZERS

Who are Baltimore's least-known national champions?

Baltimore has spawned plenty of champions in an array of sporting competitions. But there's one award-winning sports team that's surprisingly little known despite being housed in a venerable Baltimore institution.

Kennedy Krieger Institute, a Johns Hopkins affiliate, is famous enough as perhaps the nation's premier institution dedicated to improving the lives of children and young adults with pediatric developmental disabilities. But most of us are aware of it only minimally if we have never had need for its wonderful and caring services.

There is still a reason to check out the Greenspring campus—namely, the Bennett Blazers, a wheelchair basketball prep team that is a joy to watch for their awe-inspiring abilities on the court, and this was true even before they won the junior division of the 2019 National Wheelchair Basketball Championship in Chicago, defeating a team from Minnesota in the action-packed finals. (Our local champs won 48–35.)

The Bennett program provides weekly exercise and sports activities. These range from motor development for the very young to Paralympic-style training for the older athletes. Indeed,

---

Little-known fact, as far as all those championships go: Baltimore is the only city to claim four football champions in three professional leagues: Ravens and Colts in the National Football League, Stars in the US Football League, and Stallions in the Canadian Football League.

Kennedy Krieger Institute, home of the Bennett Blazers

KENNEDY KRIEGER NATIONAL CHAMPIONS

WHAT: Wheelchair basketballers

WHERE: Kennedy Krieger Institute, 3835 Greenspring Ave., Greenspring

COST: Admission cost for the tournament

PRO TIP: Blazers hold an annual tournament in the Greenspring gym. For info: bennettblazers.org/wheelchair-basketball.

Bennett alumni include the incomparable Tatyana McFadden, winner of 16 Paralympic medals, 17 IPC (World Para Athletics) World Championship medals (13 of them gold), and five New York City marathons (2010–2016).

Wheelchair basketball provides a great opportunity to check things out at the Kennedy Krieger Greenspring gym. Come to watch some great basketball and while you are at it, be awed and inspired. As the motto emblazoned on the athletes' wristbands says: "Believe and you will achieve."

BILLIE HOLIDAY ALLEY

Where can you find utterly delightful tributes to Lady Day?

South Durham Street is pretty diminutive, running north-south roughly nine blocks from Baltimore Street to Lancaster Street through the heart of Fells Point. It's a nice little residential lane, though somewhat nondescript. But turning onto South Durham from East Pratt, you'll see immediately on the eastern corner a beautiful mural of Billie Holiday stretching from the street-level doorway and shooting up three stories toward the roof; Holiday is clad in a black-and-white dress and sings into a microphone that appears cleverly incorporated into the building's rain spout.

This lovely mural would be a nice enough diversion. But turn around, because on the western side of the block, taking up one whole story from street level, is Holiday again. This time, her upper half rises, resplendent, from a bank of clouds while sun rays glow behind her. Below her is a beautiful cityscape, bisected by a flowing river—lovelier still, but we're not done.

Keep heading down Durham, and in a few more steps you'll come to yet another mural of Holiday set into the building stone: here, a mosaic of glass and ceramic (note the pieces of dinner plates that comprise the flowers in Holiday's hair). Her

---

Despite it being often reported otherwise, Holiday was not born in Baltimore (Philadelphia claims that honor). But her associations with the city are as strong, if not stronger, than with any other place, which accounts for the striking Holiday statue on the corner of West Lafayette and Pennsylvania Avenues.

BILLIE HOLIDAY TRIBUTE

WHAT: Alley decorated with Billie Holiday art

WHERE: 200 block, S. Durham St., Fells Point

COST: Free

PRO TIP: Check out the Baltimore Billie Holiday Project Facebook page.

Top: South Durham Street at Gough Street
Left: The street where Billie Holiday once lived.

face, impassioned in song, melds into a series of flying birds, one of which emerges from the glass and turns to paint upon the wooden slats that overhang the stone.

At least two more treats are just steps away: Billie Holiday memorials painted on window screens, that venerable Baltimore folk art paying tribute to a woman who spent most of her childhood in Baltimore, right here on this stretch of South Durham where she once lived.

BMA AT LEXINGTON MARKET

What do you get when you mix a venerable arts institution and the country's oldest continuous market?

To answer the question above, I'm not entirely sure (the question is somewhat rhetorical, after all, and the answer changes with the season). But it is something pretty cool.

In July 2019, the Baltimore Museum of Art opened a 250-square-foot space at Lexington Market, marrying the city's namesake art museum with the city's most famous market, which has been in continuous operation since 1782.

Let's be honest here: any discussion of Lexington Market will invite both boosters and detractors. And it's easy to understand why: You can go there one day and feel threatened and on edge (adjacent crime and homelessness) and come back the next and feel invigorated by the terrific food on offer and the buzzing, vibrant, diverse atmosphere that it projects. Consistency toward the latter is what people want, of course. And a $40 million renovation hopes to deliver just that (see sidebar).

Those who know the market already know its attractions (Faidley's, for one, whose crab cakes are widely regarded as the best in, well, the world). But for those who have opted to stay

Entrance to Lexington Market, the country's oldest market

away, Lexington Market does deserve another chance. And BMA's presence only helps. The museum space will offer special revolving exhibits, with themes based on the season. It's free and a great way to be reintroduced to an old classic—scratch that, two old classics.

Just make sure you come hungry. You're guaranteed not to leave that way.

A new South Market building will add to the 250-year-old legacy of Lexington Market, with construction completed and opening anticipated by summer 2021.

BOLTON HILL BLUE PLAQUES

How can one neighborhood have attracted so many extraordinary people?

Visitors to London in England have most likely seen numerous little blue round plaques. There are almost a thousand of them in all, marking places where various luminaries resided—famous and infamous, or sometimes obscure (Queen Victoria's dentist, for example), along with others who were internationally famed and feted (such as Mahatma Gandhi, Vincent Van Gogh, Virginia Woolf, and many others).

What a lot of people—even city locals—don't realize is that one Baltimore neighborhood has its own blue plaque program as well. A stroll around the architecturally lovely north-central neighborhood of Bolton Hill will leave you amazed by the concentration of hugely influential people who have made their homes here in the past 150-plus years.

Beginning at the 1700 block of Park Avenue, the first blue plaque, at 1729, celebrates a name not well known: Jacob Epstein. But Epstein was a philanthropist who created the system of matching charitable grants that is still in widespread use today. If this doesn't do much for you, keep walking. By the time you've checked out the neighborhood's 35 blue plaques, you'll no doubt be impressed by the list. To name just a few: President Woodrow Wilson, author F. Scott Fitzgerald, classicist Edith Hamilton, the Cone sisters, and sometime-crasher

The blue plaque program continues to expand; a dozen new plaques were nominated, researched, and installed in 2018.

1307 Park Avenue: F. Scott Fitzgerald lived here.

Gertrude Stein, whose massive bequest essentially built the Baltimore Museum of Art and funded the world's largest collection of art by Matisse. Others whose names might not be instantly recognizable but who nevertheless contributed mightily to American culture or science include the discoverer of the human biological clock, the discoverer of the anticoagulant heparin, and the inventor of the linotype (which Thomas Edison called the "eighth wonder of the world").

A LONDON-INSPIRED PLAQUE PROGRAM

WHAT: Neighborhood of luminaries

WHERE: Park Ave. and environs, Bolton Hill

COST: Free

PRO TIP: Not only is F. Scott Fitzgerald one of the blue plaque honorees, a Bolton Hill pocket park is named after him as well. A lovely green spot in an already leafy neighborhood, it sits between Wilson and Bolton Streets and Jenkins Alley.

THE BOOK THING

Are they *really* free?

The mission of The Book Thing of Baltimore is simple: "To put unwanted books into the hands of those who want them."

If you go to The Book Thing's website, there you can see the FAQs. The first three questions pretty much tell the story: Question 1: "Are the books free?"; Question 2: "Really free?"; Question 3: "Absolutely free?"; and Question 18, the last one: "And the books are free?"

So, in case you haven't yet caught on, The Book Thing gives away books—lots and lots of them. There is really only one rule: "All the books have been stamped 'not for resale' and are not to be resold. We mean it. Please honor this request." And, yeah, there is a limit to how many you can take in one day: 150,000. Seriously.

No huge surprise that a place like this exists in such a literary and quirky city. What is surprising is how many people don't know about it. But the more who do,

---

FREE BOOK STORE

WHAT: Free! Books, as many as you can carry

WHERE: 3001 Vineyard Ln., Abell/Waverly

COST: Free (that's what makes it so awesome)

PRO TIP: A complete overhaul of The Book Thing's legal and tax structure occurred in 2019–20, allowing the operation to retain its nonprofit status. But much relies on the continual use of volunteer labor; accordingly, they welcome and encourage volunteers and even have periodic volunteer training sessions.

I predict that this very book will make its way in and out of The Book Thing one day—and that would be an honor!

The Book Thing back lot, featuring a mural created by Art@Work, a mural program for Baltimore youth.

the more publicity—and books—The Book Thing gets, which means that more books are available. They're open every weekend, and the sheer number of books is astounding—and, yes, they are free. So come with a boxful of those you don't want any more and leave them there. Then, leave with a boxful of new goodies you do want.

Man, this place is awesome.

BUS STOP—LITERALLY AND FIGURATIVELY

Where can you be part of the art as you wait for your ride?

The Creative Alliance in Highlandtown has been doing its community-based art thing for decades, most prominently in the beautifully restored 1910 Patterson Theater on Eastern Avenue. It's hardly a secret. But just around the corner, on South East Avenue, is something a little less well known. It's a bus stop, which in its utilitarian ubiquity lends itself to anonymity. Except that this is no ordinary bus stop.

In fact, because it doubles as public art—made possible by grants from both the European Union National Institutes for Culture and ArtPlace America—many people are not aware that the East Avenue *B-U-S* stop is actually, well, a functioning bus stop. Instead of the standard glass cube, this stop consists of

B-U-S STOP

WHAT: Bus stop/public art

WHERE: 400 block, S. East Ave. near the intersection of Eastern Ave., Highlandtown

COST: Free (well, the bus ride costs, of course)

PRO TIP: For those with mobility challenges: the **B** was intentionally constructed to allow sitting at ground level.

Turns out that the design team behind this wonderful bus/art stop initially considered the current design as one of its first ideas, rejected it as too simple, then eventually returned to it, realizing that its simplicity was part of its charm.

Highlandtown bus stop, next to the Creative Alliance

the three letters (which, incidentally, mean the same thing in both English and Spanish, a nod to the heavily Latino neighborhood).

Meant for more than just admiring, the differing shapes of the three letters invite varying states of repose. Sit in the *U* for sky views. Crouch into the lower curve of the *S* or the lower bubble of the *B* for shelter from the rain. Kids are invariably drawn to positioning themselves in the less accessible upper *S* and *B* portions. Whatever your choice, lounging inside the 14-foot pine-plank letters is one of the more enjoyable ways to pass the time waiting for the bus.

CHESAPEAKE & ALLEGHENY STEAM PRESERVATION SOCIETY

Clams or trains? (The latter, actually.)

On the second Sunday of every month from April through November, running every 30 minutes between 11 a.m. and 3 p.m., members of the Chesapeake & Allegheny Live Steamers (CALS) provide free rides aboard miniature trains (roughly one-eighth the size of the real things). They run mostly along a 7½-inch double-tracked main line as well as elevated 4¾- and 3½-inch track lines (you don't need to have any idea what that means) on 11 acres carved out of Leakin Park. It's a pretty sweet set up: CALS leases the area from the city for a dollar a year in exchange for providing free rides to the public.

This is not for speed demons: top speeds max out at a whopping 6 mph. But that makes it perfect for the kiddoes; the two-foot average height of the train is ideal for tiny legs and arms to climb on board and grapple. That said, every ride is also jammed with adults who simply enjoy the ride, all 3,300 feet of it. And while the diminutive size of the trains makes it a tad more difficult for larger people, a ride on one of these trains affords a feeling of momentary joy while being transported to a bygone age when

CHESAPEAKE & ALLEGHENY LIVE STEAMERS

WHAT: Miniature train rides

WHERE: Windsor Mill Rd. and Eagle Dr., Leakin Park

COST: Free

PRO TIP: Donations are encouraged. After all, it costs money to keep these trains running.

CALS storage shed

things were easier and you were younger and smaller. And, hey, the sound of a steam whistle, with all its nostalgic connotations, is a thrill at any age.

The train area sits at the top of Eagle Drive. Walk the whole loop of the road, and you will pass a beautiful old miniature church, a playground, tennis courts, and—at the end of the loop—the beautiful 1856 Orianda House, as well as the outbuildings of the old Crimea Estate.

BALTIMORE'S CHINA (ER, ETHIOPIA) TOWN

Chinatown? In Baltimore?

In the 200–300 blocks of Park Avenue, between Saratoga and West Franklin Streets, remnants of what was once Baltimore's Chinatown remain in the form of distinctive Sino roofing and architectural details, as well as the occasional Chinese characters. San Francisco or New York, this is not. It's been decades since the area was a small but bustling center for Chinese culture and residents (later expanded to include multiple Asian ethnicities), centered, in part, by the Chinese Merchants Association, housed at 323-25 Park Avenue, home today to the Zhongshan Restaurant.

The area's Chinese heyday ran roughly from the late 1800s to the 1940s. But the Chinatown Collective, calling itself a "coming together of Baltimore's pan-Asian community—across ethnicity, across industry, and across generations," is working hard to resurrect the bygone glory days.

Wilson Alley, on the 400 block of Park between Franklin and Mulberry Streets, is where you'll find a large mural of a Chinese dragon and—in a nod to the changed nature of the immediate area—next to it, a mural of an Ethiopian lion, which makes

Chinatown remnants

sense as the wonderful Ethiopian restaurant, Tabor, sits nearby at 328 Park, right next door to the Abinet Ethiopian Market.

Baltimore's waves of European immigrants (the city was once second in the nation to Ellis Island as an arrival point for immigrants to the United States) have been well recorded and consistently celebrated with annual festivals and the like. This little stretch of city shines a light on Asia and a bit of Africa, too. It's well worth a visit to be part of the celebration and upswing.

In 2018, the Chinatown Collective organized the first Charm City Night Market, which attracted more than 10,000 people to Park Avenue to partake of Asian arts and foods. That success was only the beginning; the Market is now an annual event, and the group hosts smaller events throughout the year, which can be found on its website.

CARROLLTON VIADUCT

Where is the world's oldest functioning railway bridge?

Gwynns Falls Trail is a city treasure, meandering for 15 miles more or less along the serpentine Gwynns Falls in the city's northwest and running through Gwynns Falls and Leakin Parks, part of the largest unbroken urban forest in America. Traversing all 15 miles affords the walker/biker/hiker access to a bevy of wonderful sights, both natural and historic.

One of these in the latter category is the striking Carrollton Viaduct, near Carroll Park. Along a nicely wooded section of Gwynns Falls Trail, after crossing Belair Road/Wilkens Avenue and heading toward Hollins Ferry Road, the stone Carrollton Viaduct will appear on the left. It's impossible to miss. The viaduct is named after Marylander and Declaration of Independence signer Charles Carroll. When he laid the cornerstone, he remarked, "I consider this among the most important acts of my life, second only to my signing the Declaration of Independence."

Built in 1829, the bridge is 300 feet in total length with a stunning center arch with an 80-foot diameter. Baltimore is home to many railroading firsts, so it's not a huge surprise to learn that the Carrollton Viaduct was the country's first stone masonry bridge built for railroading. Because it is still in use today (talk about Old World craftsmanship!), it remains the world's oldest functioning railway bridge. President Andrew Jackson traveled on the bridge four years after its completion, making him the

---

As the trail heads under the viaduct, it follows a route that originally served as a wagon pass.

Carrollton Viaduct, the world's oldest functioning railroad bridge

first US president to ride the rails. Declared a National Historic Landmark in 1971, the Carrollton Viaduct was also named a Historic Civil Engineering Landmark 11 years later.

B&O HISTORIC STRUCTURE

WHAT: Stone railroad bridge

WHERE: Between Belair Rd., Wilmarco Ave., I-95, and South Monroe St., over Gwynns Falls

COST: Free

PRO TIP: Just to the west of the viaduct is one of the more interesting and scenic sections of Gwynns Falls Trail: a series of three steel bridges crisscrossing stone abutments of the erstwhile Brunswick Street Bridge.

THE OLDEST COLUMBUS

Did Columbus discover Baltimore?

Of course, many people will point out that Columbus didn't actually "discover" anything; after all, Baltimore's principal waterway, the Patapsco, gets its name from native Algonquian dialect. Several other tribes inhabited what is today's Baltimore region, some stretching back 12,000 years or more. Still, with the city founded by Europeans and a subsequent wave of Italians, Baltimore's love affair with Columbus makes sense.

To that end, there are three Columbus memorials in the city, one each from the 18th, 19th, and 20th centuries. For the purposes of this book, let's focus on the oldest one, as it is the least known and is located in the most obscure location of the three. It also carries with it a unique historical footnote.

This Columbus monument is fairly easy to miss: a comparatively unassuming 40-foot obelisk in a grassy area near Herring Run, where Parkside, Harford, and Argonne Roads meet. It dates to 1792 and is, amazingly, the world's oldest, still-standing monument to the explorer. When the 18th-century French consul to Baltimore, Charles-François-Adrien Le Paulmier, learned, upon the approach of the 300th anniversary of Columbus's 1492 voyage, that there were no monuments to him in this part of the world, he commissioned this statue. It was erected on his estate and stayed on that

---

In a spate of vandalism of statues of "white, dead, European males," this monument had its base smashed with a sledgehammer in 2017, rendering much of the front lettering unreadable. The obelisk, however, still stands.

Oldest Columbus monument, in Herring Run Park

land until 1964, when it was moved to where it stands today and where it now holds its world-recognized distinction.

CHRISTOPHER COLUMBUS MONUMENT

WHAT: The world's oldest monument to Christopher Columbus that is still standing

WHERE: Grassy knoll between Parkside, Harford, and Argonne Rds., Beverly Hills

COST: Free

PRO TIP: If interested, the other two Columbus monuments include a marble memorial dedicated by Ronald Reagan in 1984 in Columbus Park at the harbor across President Street from Little Italy. The other is in Druid Hill Park, copied from a statue in Genoa, Italy, and erected in 1892.

CONFEDERATE EXECUTIONS

Where in the city can one find the ghostly reminders of Civil War justice?

The house at 337 East Hamburg Street in Federal Hill is a lovely 2,600-square-foot home, with three bedrooms and two baths, and—a premium around this neighborhood—three parking spaces. And, as with many homes this old (it was built in 1810), it comes with some history: during the Civil War, it functioned as the headquarters of Union General Benjamin Butler, who would eventually serve as governor of Massachusetts. He was, before the war, a man who harbored some southern sympathies, famously declaring, "I was always a friend of southern rights but an enemy of southern wrongs." Butler's charge in 1861 was to head up the occupying forces in Baltimore, and it is here, in this East Hamburg house, where Butler lived.

While Maryland had its fair share of Confederate sympathizers (and soldiers), the

FEDERAL HILL HOUSE

WHAT: Site of Confederate soldier executions

WHERE: 337 East Hamburg St., Federal Hill

COST: Free

PRO TIP: This is a private home, so please treat it accordingly by staying on Hamburg Street and not venturing into the courtyard.

Head around the harbor and over to the President Street Station to see the sites that recorded the first casualties of the Civil War, on April 19, 1861.

The balcony where General Butler oversaw executions of Confederate soldiers

Pratt Street marker denoting the first fatalities of the Civil War

overwhelming number of Old Line fighters sided with the Union as, of course, did the state in an official capacity. Thus, the existence of a Union general in this history generally elicits good feeling. However, Butler's presence here comes with a more gruesome reality as well: it was in the basement of this house that several Confederate spies were held and where they were eventually executed in the courtyard below. It is said that Butler stood on the porch to watch the executions.

COSTUME SHOP

Which one of these is not like the others?

North Howard Street in Mount Vernon still clings to its name and reputation as Antiques Row, though—if we're being honest—the glory days that earned the 700-800 blocks that moniker are in the past. There used to be dozens of antique shops lining this strip; nowadays, there are only a handful left. That said, those that remain are still very much worth a look.

One of these shops, A.T. Jones & Sons, is not like the others. That's because it's not like anything else anywhere. Yes, there are antiques here, but A.T. Jones & Sons is first and foremost a functioning costume shop, believed to be the oldest of its kind in the country, having been around in various locations in the city for more than 150 years. The shop has supplied countless productions—movies, plays, operas, and more—over the years, and the costumes range from suits of armor to Victorian dresses to Wild West gear. Frankly, if you've seen it on the stage or the screen, they make it or it was created here.

A.T. JONES & SONS

WHAT: The country's oldest costume shop

WHERE: 708 N. Howard Street, Mount Vernon

COST: Free to visit with an appointment, but costumes vary in price

PRO TIP: Fair warning: those clown heads in the front window are pretty freaky.

It's important to note that the shop is not open for browsing. However, it's the perfect place to pick up a Halloween costume. You can make an appointment if a professional outfit is what you're after. Forget the big-box stores with their cheaply made goods; if you want the real thing, come here instead.

Front window of A.T. Jones & Sons, the country's oldest costume shop

John Waters once quipped about Charm City: "It's as if every freak in the south was headed to New York, ran out of gas in Baltimore, and decided to stay." A.T. Jones & Sons began when Alfred Thomas Jones won a painting contest hosted by MICA in 1861. He came to Baltimore from North Carolina for his $500 prize. But with the Civil War raging all around, he got stuck here. Not sure if he was a freak or not, but there are certainly shades of Waters's observation in this story.

THE COUNTRY'S FIRST STRIP MALL

Seriously? Why is this something to celebrate?

The author of this book would be the last person to heap plaudits on a strip mall. As a lover of wild, untamed places, the very idea of throwing up all that concrete and steel as a homely paean to soulless suburbia—well, I get hives at the very notion.

But the strip mall at 4800 Roland Avenue is no ordinary place. For one thing, it's architecturally lovely. Built in the 1890s and currently on the National Register of Historic Places, it's a three-story brick-and-tan Tudor beauty with a pitched roof and overlapping gables accented with distinctive timbering, calling to mind some elegant English country manor. Also consistent with the Tudor style, the mall contains tall and narrow windows composed of multiple panes. Most modern strip malls are low-slung and uninventive affairs, designed not so much for aesthetics but to place multiple storefronts in one location for ease of shopping and parking. However, on this mall, "the dominant nature of the roof takes one's eyes from the storefronts on the first floor, which are further hidden under the protecting eave of the roof. The stuccoed ends of the roof curve down from the chimneys in a manner associated with Jacobean architecture" (*National Archives Catalog*). Indeed.

ROLAND PARK MALL

WHAT: The country's first "strip mall"

WHERE: 4800 Roland Ave., Roland Park

COST: Free to look; costs to eat, obviously

PRO TIP: Two excellent restaurants make their homes in the mall: Petit Louis (French) and Johnnie's (Maryland seafood). Neither is cheap, but they both serve food of very high quality.

The country's first "strip mall," in Roland Park

The Roland Park Company, designers and overseers of that planned community, had its office in this building at the beginning, more than 130 years ago. The tenants have, of course, changed, and the trolley that used to make a U-turn here before heading back downtown is no longer running. But, blessedly, little else has changed. If only the rest of the country's strip malls looked like this.

The mall was a very intentional part of the design of what would be America's first planned community, utilizing elements developed by the City Beautiful school of landscape architecture.

CURTIS CREEK SHIP GRAVEYARD

Where can you find the disintegrating hulks of multiple ships?

If you are able and willing, paddling through Curtis Creek, a small arm connecting the Patapsco River to the southerly Marley Creek in Anne Arundel County, can be a wonderful experience. But this stretch of waterway bisects some pretty heavily industrialized shoreline, most especially along the northern reaches where it flows under the Curtis Creek drawbridge. But natural areas aren't really the main draw here. Instead, it's the hulks of dozens of boats, and the variation is striking: wooden WWI-era freighters, steam ferries, and concrete barges, to name just a few.

But you don't actually need to get on the water to see many of these sunken vessels. You can see plenty of them from the bridge on I-695. Or, better yet, make your way down to Jaws Marina off Pennington Avenue, at Walnut Point, just under the bridge on the eastern side, and walk the shoreline to see no fewer than nine old ships.

There's an American Legion Hall at Solleys Cove, on Carbide Road in Anne Arundel County. This is an excellent place to put in a small craft. A roughly two-mile paddle north toward Walnut Point will make it possible to pass by many abandoned ships not viewable from land.

The remains of two sunken ships in Curtis Creek

SUNKEN SHIPS

WHAT: Ghostly remains of dozens of ships

WHERE: Curtis Creek off Pennington Ave., Walnut Point

COST: Free

PRO TIP: Paddling the creek will allow you to move in and about some of the ships, and many of them still have prominent portions jutting out of the water, creating some fascinating sculptures.

Most of these ships came to rest here through a rather mundane history: they simply outlived their usefulness and were judged not redeemable as scrap. Thus, they were sunk here and remain today as little more than ghostly reminders of bygone days as well as mini-ecosystems for aquatic life.

But each has a history, perhaps none more interesting than the schooner *William T. Parker*. This three-masted boat was abandoned in 1899 and left in North Carolina, where it eventually drifted all the way up the eastern seaboard to Maine. There, unmanned, it drifted back south before a tugboat captured it and brought it here to Curtis Creek, where it was deliberately sunk and remains today.

DANDELION, DON'T TELL NO LIES . . .

Where can you find dandelions that will never blow away?

In the broad sweep of the Rolling Stones catalog, "Dandelion" registers with only a few hardcore Stones fans. It's a relatively obscure tune, released as a B-side in 1967 to "We Love You." It did manage to make Top Ten in the UK and Top Twenty in the US, but it quickly faded into obscurity. The lyrics include these lines: "Dandelion don't tell no lies / Dandelion will make you wise / Tell me if she laughs or cries / Blow away dandelion." Yeah, well, it was 1967.

Dandelions do blow away, of course, their seeds spreading in the wind to make . . . more dandelions. The typical median strip in Baltimore will often be full of them. And while you could conceivably make dandelion tea of their stems (it's really not very good), they are generally seen as more of a pest than anything beautiful.

But in one otherwise unassuming median in West Baltimore's Edmondson/Uplands neighborhood—specifically, where Swann Avenue and Old Frederick Road meet at Route 40—towering metal dandelions, while stationary, do seem to sway in the wind, their curvy stems leading to exploding flowery heads seemingly caught just before taking off into the breeze. Three metal-sculpture flowers grace the middle of the median,

Tonnesen's metal sculptures can be found all over the country, with similar dandelions sprouting not only in Baltimore, but in Idaho, Colorado, and Ohio, too.

Dandelion sculptures in Edmondson/Uplands

TOWERING DANDELIONS

WHAT: Metal sculptures beautifying an otherwise not-so-beautiful intersection

WHERE: Swann Ave., Old Frederick Rd., and US 40, Edmondson/Uplands

COST: Free

PRO TIP: If you want to see some natural dandelions or, better yet, more keystone foliage, the southern edge of Gwynns Falls/Leakin Park is just a half mile to the north.

while single blossoms flank either side of the road.

"The sculptures are made up of thousands of hammered stainless steel 'stars,' a reference to the many individual residents that make up the sphere of the Uplands community," the artist, David Tonnesen, was quoted as saying of the art installation. Indeed, that stainless steel has little chance of floating off. Good thing. Otherwise, this place would go back to being a boring old median strip once again instead of a temporary delight to pass through.

DICKEYVILLE

Did you land in 1800s England?

Cliché as it may sound, exploring this little-known West Baltimore village is like experiencing time and space travel. You'd be forgiven for thinking you've landed in a 19th-century English hamlet.

In fact, this area got its start much further back, in the 1670s, when trader Richard Gwynn set up a post here along the banks of Gwynns Falls to trade with native Algonquians. A village proper sprouted by 1719 with the creation of riverside mills. The construction of Franklin Paper Mill in the early 1800s led to a boom in the immediate area and then the creation of what would later become known as Dickeyville, although neighborhood welcome signs pinpoint establishment at 1772.

A distinctly Anglo feel permeates this little town, mirroring early residents' desires to have it resemble an English country village. Consequently, stone is everywhere: stone walls, stone driveways, stone gutters, and stone and Belgian block lining the streets (plus, quaint street names, such as Pickwick).

The entire village is a joy to stroll through, taking in the lovely houses—some more than 200 years old—with easy access to a mature forest in adjacent Leakin Park. But one

---

Popular author Laura Lippman, creator of, among other works, the best-selling Tess Monaghan mystery series, grew up in Dickeyville. Her 2011 novel, The Most Dangerous Thing, opens with a group of children playing kickball next to a cotton mill on Wetheredsville Road.

Welcome to Dickeyville

Pickwick Road

QUAINT CITY NEIGHBORHOOD

WHAT: An English country village transported to Baltimore's west side

WHERE: Wetheredsville, Pickwick, and Cottondale Rds., Dickeyville

COST: Free

PRO TIP: In addition to being a physically beautiful neighborhood, Dickeyville also boasts an active neighborhood association. For events, updates, and an exhaustive history, visit dickeyville.org.

particular house, at 5027 Wetheredsville Road, often stops people in their tracks. This is not one of the neighborhood's older houses, and so on a street full of them, it stands out; it was built in the 1940s and is a miniaturized replica of George Washington's home—known locally as "Little Mount Vernon." (By the way, the house next door, at 5029 Wetheredsville [circa 1850] once served as the home of the village dairy cow—seriously.)

THE DINER FROM *DINER*

Where could you once get a meal in an old film set?

It's a bit of an odd sight situated in a bit of an odd spot, there on a grassy patch with the soaring JFX above and behind it and Saratoga and Holliday Streets in front. There, a lonely, shuttered diner sits, awaiting . . . what, exactly?

Over the years it has functioned as an actual diner—serving up food and drink and welcoming all as every good diner should—until later when it became a city-owned hospitality service training ground, run alternately for city youth and for ex-offenders. But more often than not, it's been closed. So why does it still sit there, seemingly impervious to removal?

The answer to that probably has a lot to do with its nice, albeit small, place in Hollywood history. Fans of the 1982 Barry Levinson movie *Diner* (and there sure are a load of those in Baltimore) will recognize the place. Indeed, this is the actual diner from *Diner*. Originally dumped into a salvage yard in New Jersey after its life as Westbury Grill on Long Island, New York, it was rescued and reclaimed for the film. Baltimore is, and has been for some time, Ravens country.

But you will still find plenty of diehard Colts fans around, and for them, the scene in the movie in which Steve Guttenberg's fiancée must pass the arduous Colts quiz before he will marry her is a classic. Beyond that unforgettable scene, the movie presents something of a who's who of then-unknown

---

Levinson followers also know that this same diner appears in many scenes in his film Tin Men, starring Danny DeVito, Richard Dreyfuss, and Barbara Hershey.

Hollywood Diner, from the Barry Levinson movie, Diner

actors who went on to enjoy long careers in Hollywood—among them Kevin Bacon, Ellen Barkin, Tim Daly, Steve Guttenberg, Mickey Rourke, and Daniel Stern.

HOLLYWOOD DINER

WHAT: The diner that was used in the movie, *Diner*

WHERE: Saratoga and Holliday Sts., downtown

COST: Free

PRO TIP: The incomparable Baltimore Farmers Market runs every Sunday from April to December, 7 a.m.–12 p.m., below the JFX just behind the diner.

DOUGLASS TERRACE

Where did Frederick Douglass invest when he returned to Baltimore, a free man?

It may seem odd, returning to a city freely—and apparently, happily—when you were once a slave there. But after Frederick Douglass moved to Baltimore as a boy from Maryland's Eastern Shore, he viewed it as the first important milestone in his life, writing: "Going to live at Baltimore laid the foundation, and opened the gateway, to all my subsequent prosperity. I have ever regarded it as the first plain manifestation of that kind providence which has ever since attended me, and marked my life with so many favors." Despite his travails in the city, he always regarded it with something resembling fondness.

Douglass lived on Aliceanna Street in Fells Point and was employed as a ship caulker. There, he mostly taught himself to read, but he was not above playing tricks on neighborhood children or using bread to pay poor white kids to teach him. His ultimate story is well known: Douglass rose from illiterate slave to author of several essential books, earning international fame as an orator and abolitionist, and achieving the rank of US ambassador to Haiti among other accomplishments.

Later in life, he returned to Baltimore as an investor, building five houses on South Dallas Street, a stretch that today is often

FREDERICK DOUGLASS INVESTMENT PROPERTIES

WHAT: Five homes built by the famed abolitionist

WHERE: 500 block of S. Dallas St., Fells Point

COST: Free

PRO TIP: About a one-minute walk (north on Dallas, east on Eastern) is the Baltimore Tattoo Museum, well worth a visit.

500 block of South Dallas Street

referred to unofficially as Douglass Terrace. You can still see the five houses, each built from the same design and clearly distinguishable from the rest of the houses on the block.

These five houses were built specifically for African Americans in hopes of contributing to a stable community of ex-slaves and freedmen.

DRAGON BOAT CHALLENGE

Aren't dragons extinct, or not real, or . . .?

According to Wikipedia, a dragon is "a large, serpent-like legendary creature that appears in the folklore of many cultures around the world." For our purposes here, a dragon boat "is a human-powered watercraft originating from the Pearl River Delta region of China's southern Guangdong Province . . . The sport of dragon boat racing has its roots in an ancient folk ritual of contending villagers, which dates back 2000 years throughout southern China, and even further to the original games of Olympia in ancient Greece." Cool.

Today, there are dragon boat clubs and races all over the world. Not surprisingly, since Baltimore is a port city located on the second-largest natural harbor on the entire North American Atlantic seaboard, a vigorous dragon boat club exists here, too: the Baltimore Dragon Boat Club (BDBC). Begun in 2008, the club has grown to more than 100 members, ranging in age from preteens to octogenarians.

While members of the BDBC train and enter numerous races, the signature local event—the Baltimore Dragon Boat Challenge—takes place each summer and features flotilla competitions with teams of racers from up and down

---

The BDBC is open to new members, luring them with the prospective thrill of being part of a 20-person team paddling in sync through the Inner Harbor as the helmsperson steers and a drummer pounds a lively rowing rhythm.

Dragon boats in the Inner Harbor. Photo courtesy of Catholic Charities of Baltimore

the East Coast and Midwest competing along the waterfront promenade at the Under Armour headquarters in Locust Point. It's quite something to witness those narrow racing boats—crew straining at the paddles—with their intricately carved and gloriously painted dragons' heads pointing the way. Definitely an unforgettable sight and one that relatively few locals have seen.

BALTIMORE DRAGON BOAT CLUB

WHAT: Dragon boat club and racing team

WHERE: 1010 Hull St., Locust Point

COST: To join or train: first practice is free. After that, $5 per practice or $125 for the season ($75 if joining after July).

PRO TIP: The Baltimore Dragon Boat Club also has a seriously cool and informative website. Check it out: baltimoredragonboatclub.com.

DRUID AND GREEN MAN

How can termite-ridden tree stumps be transformed into amazing art?

Chainsaw sculptor Marc Acton can make it happen. Unveiled in 2012, as part of the Friends of Druid Hill Park's second annual Solstice Celebration, two 10-foot red oak stumps have lived on in the park in the Promethean forms of the extraordinary *Druid* and *Green Man*. These amazing sculptures are a testament, not only to their creator, but to the forward-thinking folks who saw potential for turning the remains of two ancient oaks into wonderful and free public art.

Druid, a bearded, gnomic figure with what appears to be an acorn cap, reposes near the northwestern edge of Druid Lake off East Drive, east of the intersection with Swann. His closed eyes, wizened cheeks, and long, flowing hair and beard imply satiety or sagacity or, frankly, anything you decide you see and interpret in his appearance.

Nearby, on a small hill on the north side of the lake,

In pagan folklore, the Green Man symbolizes the cycle of life, death, and rebirth, appearing as a person made of lush vegetation.

Green Man

Druid

Green Man has a face that was carved, fittingly, of leaves and branches, and that somehow still manages to express wisdom and the burden of the years. Where the branches and tendrils peter out at the neck, *Green Man* is fused with the lowest, untouched portions of the stump, giving the impression of a massive head emerging from the ground, still covered with and made up of natural elements.

The natural beauty of this urban park, with its serene lake and wooded walking paths, is enhanced by the whimsical and resourceful artistry of these two rugged, man-made sculptures.

EDGAR ALLAN POE'S LAST MOMENTS

Every Baltimorean knows where Poe is buried, but where did he spend his last moments?

If you want to get your Edgar Allan Poe fill in Baltimore, it makes sense to head to the Poe House and Museum on Amity Street as well as his burial place at Westminster Hall. Likewise, you could check out the gorgeous bronze statue of him in the plaza at the University of Baltimore or take in a Ravens game and watch the antics of Poe, the team mascot.

But for a different Poe pilgrimage, head instead to the outskirts of Little Italy—specifically, near the intersection of East Lombard and South High, which no doubt looks quite a bit different today than it did in the 1840s. But it was back then, in October of 1849, where Poe was discovered delirious and near death.

At the time, there was a tavern here inside Gunner's Hall, on the north side of Lombard, near the High Street intersection. Inside, the tavern was serving as a voting place as it was election day in Baltimore. It's been speculated that Poe was the victim of a common practice at the time: running indigents from polling place to polling place on the promise of a drink to vote for certain candidates. Or, possibly he was, as was presumed then, already blindingly drunk inside the tavern. Either way, he was discovered there in desperate straits.

Church Hospital, dating to 1833, closed in 2000 and subsequently became part of Johns Hopkins.

Poe's grave at Westminster Hall

POE'S DEMISE

WHAT: Where Edgar Allan Poe spent his last conscious moments

WHERE: E. Lombard near High St., Little Italy/Jonestown

COST: Free

PRO TIP: Another alleged Poe site to check out is in Fells Point at the Horse You Came In On Saloon, the oldest continually operating bar in the country, where Poe used to drink and where his ghost is said to still haunt.

A letter sent to Poe's friend attests to this: "Dear Sir,—There is a gentleman, rather the worse for wear . . . who goes under the cognomen of Edgar A. Poe, and who appears in great distress, & he says he is acquainted with you, and I assure you, he is in need of immediate assistance, Yours, in haste, Jos. W. Walker."

Alas, it was too late. Poe spent his last conscious moments here and expired at nearby Church Hospital soon after.

ELEPHANTS IN DRUID HILL

Where can you check out colorful elephant sculptures before seeing the real thing?

If driving, walking, or biking near Druid Hill Park along the outer edge to the southeast, it's easy to get distracted. First, you'd be passing the gloriously beautiful 1888 glass Victorian Rawlings Conservatory. If you then head toward Reisterstown Road on gorgeous Auchentoroly Terrace, you'll see late 19th- and early 20th-century, three-story townhomes that undulate with waved architecture splashed in vibrant colors reminiscent of the Painted Ladies in Charles Village with their corner units sprouting pyramidal roofs. And if this isn't enough, just before you reach Liberty Heights Avenue, there looms the stunning neoclassical 1921 Shaarei Tfiloh synagogue. All this awaits your pleasure amidst a backdrop of the spectacular greenery of the park.

If you've made it this far, you're ready for the pièce de résistance: five wonderful elephant sculptures installed in 2014 in an effort not only to help beautify the already beautiful neighborhood, but to encourage slower traffic as well. Look closely: these elephant sculptures, exquisitely and professionally painted, include items such as gears, hubcaps, and traffic signs to their complex designs.

The beautiful 1909 mansion on the corner of Auchentoroly Terrace and Gwynns Falls Parkway was restored and renovated in 2020 and converted into 16 apartments.

Dirt bath at Elephant Overlook

So, yes, slow down (get out of the car), and stroll along the edge of the park, taking in the two mother elephants and three babies, each totally unique.

Then, walk another half mile to the northeast, where—seemingly out of nowhere—you can see the real thing. That's because just beyond the park's Shop Road, sandwiched between tennis courts to the east and the Baltimore City Recreation and Parks Office to the west, is a slight rise, where the elephants inside the Maryland Zoo's Elephant Overlook area are visible and rather close. From that vantage point, you can watch them going for a dip or tossing dirt over their bodies with their trunks.

WORLD'S LARGEST LAND MAMMAL

WHAT: Elephants, real and constructed

WHERE: Auchentoroly Terrace/ Druid Hill Park

COST: Free

PRO TIP: If the sight of those real elephants gives you the urge to see more, the official entrance to the zoo is back a bit to the southwest, not far from where you began on Auchentoroly Terrace.

ELVIS HAS LEFT THE BUILDING . . .

But isn't that him narrating Fight Club matches?

Baltimore has had something of a love affair with Elvis Presley since he burst on the national scene. Indeed, the annual Night of 100 Elvises remains a big draw. And while Elvis-clad attendees at that event tend to favor the bloated King of the later years, plenty remember the phenomenal one-of-a-kind sleek and slick performer who took the world by storm in the mid-'50s.

ELVIS'S BIRTHDAY FIGHT CLUB

WHAT: A wacky stage performance quite unlike anything else

WHERE: Creative Alliance, 3134 Eastern Ave., Highlandtown

COST: $28 per ticket

PRO TIP: If you miss the Baltimore show, it is held annually in DC as well.

To Baltimoreans, he was still that guy in 1971 when he played the Civic Center to riotous applause and stellar reviews. Unfortunately, a return trip six years later was a different story; one reviewer wrote of his show that night: "paunchy and apparently pained, [Presley] first did 30 minutes marked by anemic singing, a few stilted attempts at his patented gyrations, bewildering patter, and awkward stage movement that included having an aide hand-hold his voice mike." Presley left the stage before the end of the show, allegedly to seek a doctor's attention. Sadly, the King would be dead just two months later.

But here in Baltimore, he lives on in part through Elvis's Birthday Fight Club, an annual event at the Creative Alliance. While the show itself is heavily advertised, the brawling participants are a closely guarded secret.

*Patterson Theater, home of
the Creative Alliance*

First, the show's backstory: Commodious, a toilet at Graceland, attempts to fulfill his dying master's last wish by setting up a "fight club" after mishearing Presley's wish for a night club. So each year, a new set of characters goes at it, with Elvis and cohost Kittie Glitter narrating the action. Previous years' matchups have included Freddy Mercury (of Queen) vs. the Queen of England, My Little Pony vs. Leatherface, Godzilla vs. Bridezilla, Diane Rehm vs. Stephen Hawking, Vladimir Putin vs. a Unicorn, Euro vs. Dollar—it gets zanier each year. So check it out—taking place annually on January 8, Elvis's birthday.

The Night of 100 Elvises is an annual event at the Lord Baltimore Hotel that raises money for various deserving charities (in case you haven't gotten enough Elvis).

EQUILIBRIUM

Where can you find public art from one of the country's hottest (and local) artists?

When Michelle Obama selected Baltimore artist Amy Sherald to create her official portrait for the Smithsonian's National Portrait Gallery, it thrust the talented artist into the national spotlight. The former First Lady's choice was an inspired one, and the resulting portrait did not disappoint. In fact, when it first went on display, it had to be moved to a larger space to accommodate the public's overwhelming interest in seeing it. And no wonder: it's a striking painting, employing Ms. Sherald's signature style of rendering African American skin tones in shades of gray while clothing her subjects in bold mosaics of color.

Unsurprisingly, since then Ms. Sherald's work has been in great demand. Lucky for us locals, she lives and produces here, and, even luckier for us, she feels an affinity with her home city. So when it came time to create a wall-sized mural of her painting *Equilibrium*, the Parkway Theater, near Ms. Sherald's home studio, became the lucky designated location. Said the artist: "I am excited to unveil this mural of *Equilibrium* in Baltimore, in a community so foundational to my portraits of Black Americans. To situate this piece along North Avenue, the electric nerve of our city, blocks away from my studio, is to return my artwork to the central muse of my creative practice for over a decade."

If you're ever at the US Embassy in Dakar, Senegal, you can see the original painting, part of the embassy's permanent collection.

Equilibrium

AMY SHERALD'S
EQUILIBRIUM

WHAT: Mural on the Parkway Theater

WHERE: 5 W. North Ave., Station North

COST: Free

PRO TIP: While checking out the art outside the Parkway, don't hesitate to look inside this venerable old theater, too. Built in 1915, its recent restoration means it is back to showing a wonderful selection of films in its original glory.

Equilibrium depicts a woman balancing a pole and a heart on a chain; present, too, are the artist's trademark gray skin tones and colorful clothing, all against a striking red-and-orange background. It is, without question, a wondrously large reminder of what a truly visionary artist Amy Sherald is.

FACTORY OF CHAMPIONS

What unassuming building has churned out multiple Olympians?

Since the 1984 Olympic Games in Los Angeles, eleven swimmers who trained with the North Baltimore Aquatic Club have competed in the Olympics. Together, they have racked up an astonishing number of medals: 34 golds, eight silvers, and seven bronzes. Additionally, the NBAC has been the training ground for three Paralympians, including the incomparable Jessica Long, who is the second-most decorated US Paralympian of all time having earned 23 Paralympic medals.

Of course, these impressive numbers are buttressed by the fact that the NBAC was the longtime home of the most decorated Olympian, in any sport, in history: Michael Phelps, who grew up in nearby Rodgers Forge and who, over the course of five Olympic Games, accrued 28 medals, 23 of them gold.

The NBAC trains its athletes at several locations in and around North Baltimore. But because of Phelps and the fact that it was in the unassuming Meadowbrook Swim Club where he developed into one of history's greatest athletes, it is this spot in Mount Washington that is most associated with his glorious record. You'll find surprisingly little visible at Meadowbrook to trumpet this illustrious history—though much focus is given to continuing the legacy. The vast majority of visitors drive right past it and head, instead, to the wonderful early 19th-century

---

In addition to all those medals, NABC swimmers also hold 48 world records.

Mount Washington Mill

Mill complex that houses many terrific stores, including the anchor, Whole Foods. But if you turn left instead of heading to the Mill, there you will find Meadowbrook, just across the way from the Mount Washington post office. Unless you were in the know, you'd never know it was there.

MEADOWBROOK SWIM CLUB/NBAC

WHAT: Once training ground to Michael Phelps and other Olympians

WHERE: 5700 Cottonworth Ave., Mount Washington

COST: None, though you do need to be a member to swim there (or come as a guest of a member); memberships range from $430 to $865 per season.

PRO TIP: As mentioned, the Mount Washington Mill complex is in the same general area as Meadowbrook. There's a Starbuck's, a Whole Foods, an ice cream concession, a wine shop, and more, all housed in a lovely refurbished cotton mill complex built in 1807. Of the buildings you can still see today, the oldest is the Stone Mill, from 1811.

FLAG HOUSE (NO, NOT THAT ONE)

Where can you find one seriously massive representation of the beloved state standard?

The Star Spangled Banner Flag House in Little Italy is a wonderful museum, housed in an 18th-century home and depicting the lives of the Pickersgill family. They, along with 13-year-old indentured servant Grace Wisher, gained fame for sewing the flag that was ultimately raised over Fort McHenry and inspired Francis Scott Key to write "The Star-Spangled Banner."

Nowadays, the country has 50 state flags, plus flags for Washington, DC, and five US territories. I'm a Marylander, so, sure, go ahead and accuse me of bias. But the Maryland flag is, quite simply, the country's best. Its bold four-quadrant design and unique color pattern is a standout against any flag in the world (though, for my money, the flags of Mozambique, Uganda, Wales, and Bhutan come pretty darn close).

A visit to this neighborhood should involve more than just gawking at this flag house. Within a few walkable blocks are incredible restaurants (notably, the Food Market, Grano's, and the iconic Café Hon, among others), great shops (including Bazaar, covered in this book), and Atomic Books, where John Waters regularly drops in to pick up his mail.

Maryland flag on Baltimore in a Box

BALTIMORE IN A BOX RETAIL STORE

WHAT: The Maryland flag covering a two-story rowhouse

WHERE: 857 W. 36th St., Hampden

COST: Browsing is free. Boxes containing things iconic to Baltimore range from $49 to $125.

PRO TIP: You can see a series of photographs documenting the painting of the house on the store website: baltimoreinabox.com.

While the Maryland flag has always enjoyed a prominent place in our state—flying atop the country's oldest continuous capital in Annapolis, for example—it has become more ubiquitous in recent years. You'll find proud denizens sporting the Calvert and Cross standards on shirts, shorts, socks, headbands, scarves—the list goes on. You'll see it on the backs of cars and sometimes even painted on them, as well as integrated into the uniforms of the Ravens and the Orioles. Watching as the massive flag is unfurled during University of Maryland athletic events is an awesome experience.

But if you want to check out the majesty of an entire two-story rowhouse covered top to bottom in the glorious pattern, head to The Avenue in Hampden (36th Street), to the retail store Baltimore in a Box, to gaze in wild wonder at the "other flag house."

FLOAT LIKE A BUTTERFLY, STING LIKE A BEE

Where is the mecca of Baltimore's proud boxing scene?

While Baltimore isn't recognized nationally as a mecca for boxing champions, the city has had its fair share, going all the way back to the 19th century, with local Joe Gans leading the pack. Gans may not conjure immediate recognition, but he has been hailed as the greatest lightweight boxer of all time by multiple boxing historians. Gans was the first African American world boxing champ of the 20th century and held his title as World Lightweight Champion from 1902 to 1908. Today, a bronze statue of him graces the lobby at Madison Square Garden.

More recently, Baltimore has produced champions in Nick Kisner (a multiple cruiserweight champion) and Hasim Rahman (two-time world heavyweight champion) and, most recently, Gervonta Davis, a two-time super featherweight world champion. Davis retained his title with a second-round TKO at Royal Farms Arena in a spectacular homecoming in July of 2019, marking the first time since 1940 that a Baltimore

UPTON BOXING CENTER

WHAT: Home of Baltimore boxers, champions and otherwise

WHERE: 1901 Pennsylvania Ave., Upton

COST: Boxing club: $120 yearly membership/ $5 drop-in

PRO TIP: The Upton Boxing Center sits within the Pennsylvania Avenue Black Arts and Entertainment District, furthering the momentum to reclaim some of the old glory days when this area rivaled New York on the famed Chitlin' Circuit.

Upton Boxing Center, community anchor and home of champions

native had a world title bout in his home city. It is the fact that Davis's home gym is the Upton Boxing Center that has shined a spotlight on this neighborhood resource.

In addition to the obvious boxing-related accoutrements, the center also provides computers and a work area for kids to do their homework. According to the center's promotional material, "The Upton Boxing Center has become a mecca for local amateur boxing by developing state, regional and national champions in youth and young adult age groups. Participants in the nationally recognized Upton boxing program come from all over the region because of the tremendous instruction, mentoring and camaraderie."

Davis echoed the sentiment in his comments about the Upton Center: "I was taken away from my family when I was young, so just having that atmosphere, being around that crowd, it helped me a lot. That's why I was passionate to come to the gym. It was boxing, but it wasn't really boxing. It was the love."

In its first decade of operation, Upton has produced 15 boxers, male and female, who have won at least one championship tournament or match.

FRANK ZAPPA'S HEAD

How did this thing end up here?

Perched atop a 12-foot pole in front of the Southeast Anchor branch of Enoch Pratt Library sits a bronze sculpture of Frank Zappa's head. The story of how and why it arrived here is as unique as the man himself.

First, a bit about Zappa the musician: During a career that lasted more than 30 years, he produced and recorded some 60 albums either as a solo artist or with his band, the Mothers of Invention. He was also among a group of musicians who memorably argued for First Amendment rights before a 1985 Senate subcommittee considering music censorship, providing the most impassioned and eloquent testimonial of the bunch. He was inducted into the Rock and Roll Hall of Fame in 1995 and won a Lifetime Achievement Grammy in 1997.

The story of the Frank Zappa bust's journey to Baltimore begins in Vilnius, Lithuania. After Lithuania's break from the Soviet Union, the citizenry began removing busts of Soviet luminaries that dotted the city. The Vilnius chapter of the Frank Zappa Fan Club commissioned a sculptor who used to create busts of Stalin to do one of Zappa and had it installed to great fanfare: President Vaclav Havel presided over the dedication, and a military brass band played renditions of Zappa songs.

The Lithuanian nonprofit organization ZAPPART offered a replica of that bust to Baltimore, the city of Zappa's birth, in

BRONZE HEAD

WHAT: Bust of Frank Zappa

WHERE: 3601 Eastern Ave., Highlandtown

COST: Free

PRO TIP: If you find yourself in Lithuania, the Zappa bust is in a courtyard off K. Kalinausko g. 3, Vilnius 03107, a 10-minute walk from the Museum of Occupations and Freedom Fights.

Enoch Pratt Free Library
Southeast Anchor Branch

Frank Zappa bust in front of the Southeast Anchor Branch of Enoch Pratt Free Library

The original sits in Vilnius, Lithuania.

2008. The mayor of Vilnius at the time endorsed the idea, writing, "I hope that replication of the original statue of Frank Zappa in Vilnius and bringing it to Baltimore will perpetuate the memory of one of the greatest artists of the century." It was dedicated on Frank Zappa Day, in 2010, and it's been there ever since, gazing out at the citizens of the place where he was born.

Rolling Stone magazine ranked Frank Zappa in its "100 Greatest Artists of All Time" (at #71, just ahead of AC/DC and just behind The Police).

FREE CONCERTS

Where can you hear students "shape the future of music"?

Like many things associated with the Johns Hopkins University, the Peabody Institute is a transformational place. Named for its benefactor, George Peabody, the institute was founded in 1857, making it "the first major intellectual and arts center in an American city" and taking its place within a wave of local philanthropy that saw the creation of the Walters Art Gallery, the Johns Hopkins University, and the Enoch Pratt free library system, bedrock Baltimore institutions to this day. The Peabody has been affiliated with Johns Hopkins since the late 1970s and, as such, enjoys the tremendous resources of such a partnership. It is today widely regarded as one of the leading music conservatories in the nation.

And here's how you can be a beneficiary: first, check out the Peabody's calendar of events on its website (see below), and choose from a wide slate of recitals open to the public. Most of these are given by Peabody students, who are required to perform public recitals. Each of these students was attracted to the institute by its promise (and, quite often, the realization of that promise) to, in the words of the institution "shape the future of music."

Make sure to leave time to duck next door and check out the Peabody Library and whatever exhibit is currently on display there. The library is quite simply one of the most spectacular public spaces anywhere.

Peabody entrance

The recitals generally last an hour and range from all classes of instruments to vocals as well, encompassing multiple musical genres. Trust me on this one: these students are *good*, and would be worth a cost of admission. But, as noted, the concerts are all free.

PEABODY CONSERVATORY

WHAT: Free concerts at one of the top music schools in the country. View concert dates and times for the Peabody Institute at hub.jhu.edu/events.

WHERE: 1 E. Mount Vernon Place, Mount Vernon

COST: Free

PRO TIP: Mount Vernon Square is magnificent, easily in the running for the most beautiful public square in the country. It also hosts a number of interesting sites, but just across the street from the Peabody is the stunning Mount Vernon Place United Methodist Church, a Victorian Gothic beauty, completed in 1872. Francis Scott Key died on this spot in 1843 when the Charles Howard mansion stood here (1830). His body was moved in 1866 to his family's ancestral home, Terra Rubra in Carroll County.

GAS LIGHTING (TWO WORDS, NOT ONE)

Where is the country's first (and maybe last) municipal gas light?

Sometime around 2018, as a reflection of the country's political climate, the term *gaslighting*, meaning to manipulate someone into questioning his or her own sanity, entered the popular lexicon. Steering clear of the political bent here, gas lighting as a historical phenomenon created a radical change in the way people interacted with their environments in cities and towns.

Consider: one could suddenly walk at night and actually see beyond the paltry illumination of a handheld candle. Though, to be fair, some cities did employ outdoor lighting; it's just that the lights usually used whale oil, which was smokier and stinkier than gas and required on-site fill-ups. Gas lighting was a major improvement.

And it all began on the corner of today's Baltimore and Holliday Streets in 1817. In fact, the first gas lighting was used in 1816 by Rembrandt Peale to attract visitors to his new museum on Holliday Street. It was a sensation, and almost immediately the Baltimore City Council created the Gas Light Company of Baltimore. The city began to lay pipes for the municipal gas system, ultimately beginning at this corner with the first lamp,

---

GAS LIGHT MARKER

WHAT: Site of the country's first municipal gas lamp

WHERE: East Baltimore and Holliday Sts., downtown

COST: Free

PRO TIP: While the existing fixture isn't original, the pole is, somehow surviving the purge when gas lighting was phased out; after World War I, the city began replacing the gas lights with electric, with the last one gone by 1957.

America's first municipal gas lamp

The Peale Museum

Peale's demonstration of gas lighting as imagined by painter McGill Mackall in 1803

This structure is the oldest museum building in the United States. Designed by Robert Cary Long, Sr. for Rembrandt Peale, the museum opened to the public in 1814 as "an elegant Rendezvous for taste, curiosity and leisure." For a 25-cent admission fee, Baltimoreans came to admire "birds, beasts, antiquities and miscellaneous curiosities" as well as paintings by members of the Peale family.

The audience was dazzled on June 11, 1816, when Rembrandt Peale illuminated the museum with burning gas. This feat led to the founding the same year of The Gas Light Company of Baltimore, the first commercial gas company in the country.

In 1830, the City bought the museum for use as the first City Hall. In 1878 the building served as a public school for African American children.

William Donald Schaefer, Mayor
Rededicated 2005 Martin O'Malley, Mayor

Baltimore City Landmark
National Historic Landmark

Historical marker denoting the birth of gas lighting at the Peale Museum

which is memorialized by the pole and lamp that still stands there today.

What's fascinating to consider is that this is not only the country's first municipal gas light, and one that stays on perpetually. It is also, ironically, one of the last functioning city gas lights in the United States.

At the time the first gas lighting took place, Baltimore and Holliday Streets were known as Market and Lemon.

GRAFFITI ALLEY

Should you bring along your own spray cans?

Yes, you should—bring your cans, that is. That's the point: openly sanctioned and encouraged "vandalism." Or you can simply take in the splendor. And keep visiting; it changes by the day. Indeed, Graffiti Alley regularly attracts visitors and artists eager to make their own marks.

This is a section of the city that not so long ago was teetering on the edge of being a no-go zone. That has changed with the influx of art and artists who now inhabit the blocks north of Penn Station, logically dubbed Station North. Theaters, galleries, art spaces, murals—the area buzzes with creative energy.

And this alley off Howard Street is a perfect microcosm of that vibe. A decade ago, the safety conscious might have given this alley a wide berth; but now, because of the change in atmosphere and the constant state of artistic renewal, it's a great place to go to take in the ever-changing visual explosion.

ALLEY ART

WHAT: Sanctioned space for graffiti art

WHERE: Howard St. and W. 19 ½ St., Station North

COST: Free

PRO TIP: It is expected and accepted that existing art will be sprayed over, so don't feel compelled to hunt for an empty space (there really aren't any, anyway). However, the established practice is to leave alone works deemed superior.

It's quite common to witness locals—and not-so-locals—using the paint-covered brick walls as a backdrop for photos and video shoots.

Women using Graffiti Alley as a backdrop

And kudos to city officials who, instead of taking the heartless position that graffiti, in whatever form, is vandalism, have recognized that this is public art that attracts creative types, plus visitors who simply want to soak it in. In revitalizing this area, they have acknowledged that some graffiti is good for the city and that it contributes to Baltimore's already well-earned reputation as an arts hub.

Come on by; the atmosphere and energy are safe and electric.

GREAT BALTIMORE OYSTER PARTNERSHIP

Doesn't an oyster sanctuary sound nice?

The above question comes from the Great Baltimore Oyster Partnership, a consortium of groups and individuals partnering with the Chesapeake Bay Foundation. And, to answer: yes, it does. While true believers adore the taste (and feel) of slurping down a good local oyster, these bivalves can be a tough gustatory sell for others. Let's face it: they don't look or feel terribly appetizing as they slither down one's throat, even with a dollop of cocktail sauce or lemon and accompanied by a beautiful oyster stout. But you need not want to eat oysters to appreciate the work they do.

The oyster's ability to clean water is extraordinary. An adult can filter 50 gallons a day. Multiply that by a few billion oysters, and you get an infinitely cleaner Chesapeake Bay.

Unfortunately, we're far removed from the days when an estimated trillion oysters filled the bay, filtering the country's largest estuary in a mere three days. With today's drastically decreased population—estimated at roughly a billion, which sounds like a lot but is only 1 percent of historic highs—it takes the bay's current oyster population more than a year to do the same job.

OYSTER REVIVAL

WHAT: Helping increase Chesapeake Bay's vital oyster population

WHERE: Locations vary.

COST: Free

PRO TIP: Learn more by visiting the Chesapeake Bay Foundation website at http://www.cbf.org and searching for Great Baltimore Oyster Partnership.

Oyster caretaking location in Canton

Oysters, pre-shucked

So here's your chance to help. From fall to summer, oyster gardens are tended at sites along the harbor. Then the oysters are taken to a sanctuary in the Patapsco. And you can help make it happen by tending to the maturing bivalves.

Two Saturday mornings per month, individuals can join the Great Baltimore Oyster Partnership by helping to install and maintain oyster gardens in Canton and Federal Hill. Doing this under-the-radar but immensely important work will help to realize the ultimate goal of adding 10 billion oysters to the bay by 2025.

Oyster reefs have been shown to act as a natural defense against the ravages of coastal storm surges. So do what you can—even if the idea of eating them still gives you the willies.

HANSA HAUS

Where did some of the country's worst domestic terrorist attacks get planned?

At Charles and Redwood Streets is a unique, beaux-arts building that stands out from everything else on the block. It was built in 1912 and was originally designed as the headquarters of North German Lloyd and Hamburg American Steamship lines. In addition to being of generally beautiful construction, it retains some stunning architectural details, such as the exquisite coat of arms near the top of the pitched roof; this is a reflection of the Hanseatic League, a confederation of merchant guilds from northern Europe— *hansa* loosely meaning *convoy*—to delineate the merchants traveling between the confederated cities. Thus, this old beauty is known as Hansa Haus.

It was in this house that German saboteurs plotted successful explosions in two locations. One was the Black Tom attack in New York Harbor in 1916, resulting in the destruction of half a billion dollars' worth of munitions and causing an explosion so large and furious that it damaged the Statue of Liberty. A historical marker at the site today reads, "You are walking on a site which saw one of the worst acts of terrorism in American history" and claims that "the noise of the

---

The location of Hansa Haus in this spot is no accident. This area's German influence before WWI was so strong that Redwood Street actually used to be named German Street before wartime sentiment called for a renaming.

1912 Hansa Haus

BEAUX-ARTS BEAUTY WITH A DARK PAST

WHAT: Site of planned 19th-century terrorist attacks

WHERE: 11 S. Charles St., Downtown

COST: Free

PRO TIP: Just next door to Hansa Haus is the Greek-inspired Ionic Temple, originally built for the Savings Bank of Baltimore. And just beyond that is the corner of Charles and Baltimore, significant because this is the spot from which all city streets—east, west, south, and north—are calculated.

explosion was heard as far away as Maryland and Connecticut." Also planned at Hansa Haus was the Kingsland explosion in Lyndhurst, New Jersey, in 1917, where 1,400 factory workers barely managed escape before the place blew sky high.

The planners of these acts of terrorism also hatched similar schemes for later use in Baltimore, including inciting dock workers and placing bombs filled with anthrax and glanders. Fortunately, these never came off.

HEBREW ORPHAN ASYLUM

Why would a repurposed asylum be a good idea?

As the Jewish population of the city grew in the 19th century, the Hebrew Benevolent Society of Baltimore was established and eventually oversaw the creation of the Hebrew Orphan Asylum. At the dedication, German Jewish merchant William S. Rayner, a driving force in the asylum's creation, declared: "The Jewish community should regard donations as an investment that would bear fruit; some of the children in the future would contribute to the welfare of the community, and the rest would serve as the contributor's advocates in heaven." The asylum would serve the community and its children until its closure in 1923.

In May of 2019, the Hebrew Orphan Asylum got some love in the form of reinforced steel—the beginning of a total $17 million reconstruction of this magnificent old building that had been abandoned some three decades earlier and that has been the focus of a 16-year effort to save it. Its roof had long since collapsed and its windows had been boarded up, despite

---

Much like the spectacular American Brewery building in Broadway East, it's heartening to know that yet another wonderful old structure will no longer be left to collapse in Baltimore but will get a new life built upon the foundations of the old: serving the community in which it stands.

The Hebrew Orphan Asylum after the scaffolding came down

receiving a much-deserved listing on the National Register of Historic Places in 2010.

Before restoration and in spite of the long-term neglect, this grand old Romanesque Victorian castle, which occupied much of the 2700 block of Rayner Avenue between Ashburton and Dukeland, still inspired awe as it loomed over the street. Constructed in 1876 of red brick, with turrets and multiple-story wings, it remains an impressive building. After its restoration is complete, it will house offices of Baltimore Health Department and the Behavioral Health System Baltimore, along with those of other community health-care providers.

STONY RUN (page 176)

GRAFFITI ALLEY (page 80)

PEABODY LIBRARY (page 76)

BILLIE HOLIDAY ALLEY (page 22)

DANDELION SCULPTURES (page 48)

NATIONAL MUSEUM OF DENTISTRY (page 106)

A.T. JONES & SONS (page 42)

PENNSYLVANIA AVENUE BLACK ARTS AND ENTERTAINMENT DISTRICT (page 180)

NATIONAL AQUARIUM (page 178)

BABE RUTH'S HOUSE (page 12)

DRAGON BOAT CHALLENGE (page 56)

ROLAND PARK PATHS (page 162)

BATTLE MONUMENT (page 134)

HOUSE OF PAIN

What were George Washington's dentures really made of?

Sitting next door to each other are two sites perfect for those with an interest in medical history (but which might not be so attractive to those who are squeamish about the human body).

First up is the delightfully quirky National Museum of Dentistry, sitting within the University of Maryland, Baltimore medical campus. Here, you will find out more than you probably ever wanted to know about oral health (or the lack thereof). This is especially apropos because the University of Maryland School of Dentistry was the world's first dental college and loaned many of its artifacts to the museum. A typical display recounts George Washington's awful relationship with his teeth, even including a pair of his dentures (ivory, not wood, as the legend is often told).

It was in Anatomical Hall where the Revolutionary War hero, Frenchman, and George Washington confidante, the Marquis de Lafayette, was awarded the University of Maryland's first honorary doctorate in 1824.

Davidge Hall, America's oldest medical education building

When done, head next door to Davidge Hall, which has been used as a medical education building since it was built in 1812—making it the oldest building of its kind in the Western Hemisphere. A riot a few years prior to its establishment, by citizens concerned that human dissection was tantamount to desecration, led to a burned building and, more important, the hasty establishment thereafter of an officially sanctioned medical school where cadaver dissections could take place under more acceptable conditions.

The building itself is a beauty, built to last for centuries and with two imposing amphitheaters (called Chemical and Anatomical Halls). Above, the domed roof displays intricate patterns that are reminiscent of buildings in older European capitals.

IRISH RAILROAD WORKERS MUSEUM

There's another museum near the B&O?

Sure is. Part of the obscurity of this museum is that it sits almost literally in the shadow of the immense and internationally known B&O Railroad Museum. Built on the spot of the first commercial rail line in the United States, the B&O possesses "the oldest, most historic and most comprehensive American railroad collections in the world." Loads of people check out this amazing museum. But the vast majority of those visitors then go on to other things. Too bad, because the Irish Railroad Workers Museum is just one block north on Lemmon Street.

In the 1840s, at the time of the Irish potato famine, Baltimore saw a large influx of émigrés from the Emerald Isle. Many settled in this neighborhood and worked for the railroads. The museum celebrates and illuminates that history inside five alley houses, 912-920 Lemmon (the Irish flags are a giveaway), with the exhibits concentrated in 918-920. Inside one 12-foot-wide house, originally built in 1848 and sold for $400, you can follow the story of the Feeley family and get a good sense of what life was like here for this immigrant family more than 150 years ago. With immigration a heated contemporary political topic, this is a wonderful museum for getting a little perspective on the past and the present.

IRISH WORKERS MUSEUM

WHAT: Museum celebrating the lives of Irish families in Baltimore in the 19th century

WHERE: 918 Lemmon St., SOWEBO

COST: Free

PRO TIP: Visits to the museum are free and private tours can be arranged in advance. Registration takes place at the B&O Museum.

Irish Railroad Workers Museum and Shrine

By the beginning of the 21st century, those of Irish ancestry made up almost 15 percent of the Baltimore-area population, second only to citizens of German descent.

JOSEPH KAVANAGH CO., PRACTICAL COPPERSMITHS

How did an old coppersmith company come to serve as a front for bootlegging?

Today, Harbor East is a glittering jewel on the Baltimore cityscape, a place unrecognizable to any Baltimorean who left a decade or so ago and hasn't been back. What was once a grimy industrial expanse is now a collection of high-end restaurants, hotels, and offices. But a short walk north from Harbor East on South Central Avenue will bring you to a relic of bygone days.

At 201 South Central, and wrapping around the corner onto East Pratt, stands an old, three-story brick building, once home to Joseph Kavanagh Company, Practical Coppersmiths. The company itself is no longer here, having moved out to Dundalk to continue the family tradition of metalworking that was started at the Central Avenue location in 1866.

Any company around for more than 150 years will, of course, have had good times and bad. But what makes this story interesting was a bad time around 1920 when the metalworks business was taking a hit. Those were good times, though, for making money off Prohibition. Kitty, a younger-generation Kavanagh, married the notorious gangster Jack

Jack Hart's penchant for escaping penitentiaries earned him the nickname "Prison Houdini."

110

Old bootlegging site

OLD COPPERSMITHS BUILDING

WHAT: Bootlegging front

WHERE: 201 S. Central Ave., Jonestown

COST: Free

PRO TIP: The building is boarded up now, but to see evidence of its old use, move to the Pratt Street side. The words "Joseph Kavanagh Co." run horizontally at the top of the building, while "Practical Coppersmi" runs vertically toward the street (the "th" in "coppersmith" has faded out).

Hart, who was an old hand at bootlegging, and the business started churning out whiskey at this location on Central Avenue. Hart spent the next decade in and out of prisons, but when the Depression hit, the operation started up again full force. By then, the physical plant had moved to Lakewood Avenue in Canton, where Hart and the Kavanaghs made and bootlegged gin and rye, sustaining the family business beyond the end of Prohibition until the mid-1930s.

And while the venerable—and completely legit—family business continues today on Lynhurst Road in Baltimore County, the old brick building north of Harbor East provides a tangible reminder of a different kind of business, long ago and thoroughly of another era.

KITE CELEBRATION

Will It Fly?

New in 2019, and promising to become a Baltimore springtime tradition, the Big Baltimore Kite Fest is the brainchild of the folks at Creative Alliance, who have teamed up with yet another city resource gem, the Friends of Patterson Park. What a wonderfully simple and wonderfully wonderful idea: invite the city out to Patterson Park, "Baltimore's Backyard," to participate in that most breezy and colorful outdoor activity that resonates with carefree childhood delight, flying a kite.

Participants are encouraged to bring their own kites, but you can purchase or, even better, make one on site. Of course, there are also food, drink, music, and face-painting booths, along with kite-flying demonstrations and more—not to mention access to the beautiful Patterson Park Pagoda. The only rule: all kites must be acoustic (in other words, nothing motorized, such as drones).

BIG BALTIMORE KITE FEST

WHAT: Annual kite-flying/-making festival

WHERE: Patterson Park, 2601 E. Baltimore St.

COST: If you wish to make your own kite at the festival, a $5 donation is suggested for materials.

PRO TIP: Because Patterson Park is so often bustling and is hemmed in by densely populated neighborhoods, parking can be a challenge during event days. Consider using MTA; buses run frequently along Eastern Avenue, on the park's southern border.

In keeping with the nonmotorized theme, the festival has wind-powered non-amplified music going all day long.

Patterson Park Pagoda

Topping it all off is the Will It Fly? competition. Folks are encouraged to put up the most creative thing they can design and see if it will fly. It must have a string, can't be a traditional kite, can't have a motor, and must stay aloft for at least 20 seconds. Other than that, the sky—and your imagination—are the limits.

What a terrific way to usher in spring.

G. KRUG & SON

There are still blacksmiths?

Indeed there are. And the oldest continually operating one in the United States is right here in Baltimore, on Saratoga Street. In 1810, German immigrant Augustus Schwatka began the blacksmith shop at 415 West Saratoga, and it has been supplying metalworks—from the mundane to the ornate— to residents and businesses ever since. Forty years after its founding in 1850, Gustav Krug emigrated from Germany and joined the business, eventually taking over in 1871.

G. Krug & Son is still an operating metalworks, of course, but it is also a functioning museum, opening its doors to visitors who wish to learn about its history and techniques. The Krugs, according to their website, want to showcase a "history that is little known, but is literally everywhere you look in the city." Indeed, as Theodore Krug II says, "There is hardly a building in Baltimore that doesn't contain something we made, even if it is only a nail."

True enough, creations from the Krugs adorn virtually every block, right down to the ubiquitous fire escapes. But some of their output is even more conspicuous: animal cages at the Maryland Zoo; the gating and fencing at Johns Hopkins, both the university and the hospital; and the gating at Greenmount Cemetery, to name just a few. And the influence isn't just in Charm City. All up and down the East Coast, G.

METALWORKS

WHAT: The country's oldest continually operating blacksmith shop

WHERE: 415 W. Saratoga St., Downtown

COST: None to visit; costs for a wide range of custom metalwork and restoration work do vary.

PRO TIP: Tours are given Monday-Friday from 7 a.m. to 3 p.m. To schedule, call 410-752-3166.

Home of a venerable old blacksmith, the country's oldest

Krug & Son has made its mark at places such as the Museum of Modern Art in New York City and the Home of the Commandants in Washington, DC.

Lexington Market (see page 24) is just half a block to the southwest, down Paca Street.

LONDON COFFEE HOUSE

Where do good ideas come from?

Built in 1771, the structure at the corner of South Bond and Thames Streets in Fells Point has been dramatically repurposed. Some of us longer-tenured Baltimoreans might remember the days when this building was little more than a lonely façade standing sentinel on the outermost edge of Fells Point. Wonderfully, that façade wasn't torn down but rather incorporated into the building you see there now. Older than the country itself, this building has an important historical distinction: it was the country's last colonial-era coffeehouse still standing.

In the 2010 *TED* talk, "Where Do Good Ideas Come From?" writer Steven Johnson hailed the coffeehouse as a major driver in the birth of the Enlightenment, explaining that before the coffeehouse, most folks drank alcohol all day long because the water could not be trusted. As he noted: "Until the rise of the coffeehouse, you had an entire population that was effectively drunk all day. And you can imagine . . . if you were drinking all day, and then you switched from a depressant to a stimulant, you would have better ideas. You would be sharper and more alert. And so it's not an accident that a great flowering of innovation happened as England switched to tea and coffee."

Thames is meant to invoke London's famous river, but Baltimoreans know this street with a different pronunciation than London's "Tems." Around here, it's usually "Thames" with a soft th and a long a. You'll hear both.

The restored London Coffee House, today headquarters of Canusa Corporation

FORMER HOME OF THE LONDON COFFEE HOUSE

WHAT: Colonial-era hangout spot

WHERE: Corner of Thames and South Bond Sts., Fells Point

COST: Free

PRO TIP: You could spend all day wandering around Fells Point and gawking at all the historical buildings. But if you just want some good old vinyl (plus tons of other goodies), head to Soundgarden, the city's best record shop located just a few hundred meters east on Thames.

A colonial export to the Americas, the coffeehouse functioned similarly here. As for this one in Fells Point, the London Coffee House is where pre-Revolutionary patriots met to discuss the coming insurrection against the British. The building also has the distinction of being Fells Point's oldest commercial structure.

LOVELY LANE UNITED METHODIST CHURCH

Where was American Methodism founded?

It's quite well known and celebrated that Baltimore is more or less the birthplace of Catholicism in this part of the planet: The extraordinary Baltimore Basilica in Mount Vernon was the first Catholic cathedral in the New World.

Mother Seton House, in Seton Hill, was the home of Elizabeth Ann Seton, the first American canonized as a saint. Adjacent to her home is St. Mary's Seminary, the oldest Catholic higher-learning institution in the country. Seton also established and ran the country's first free school for girls and established the country's first order of nuns. Likewise, Baltimore saw the institution of the first African American Catholic community of nuns in the United States, the Oblate Sisters, created in 1829 by Haitian immigrant Mary Elizabeth Lange.

But fewer folks know about the historical significance of Lovely Lane United Methodist Church, which is also known as the Mother Church of American Methodism. Baltimore has that distinction because Lovely Lane is the principal church of a congregation that began here in 1784, making it America's first Methodist church and mirroring the held-over social and cultural split between the fledgling colonies and England.

As for that name: there is a Lovely Lane in Baltimore (well, there are many lovely lanes in Baltimore), but the actual "Lovely Lane" is an alley in Bolton Hill linking John and Rutter Streets.

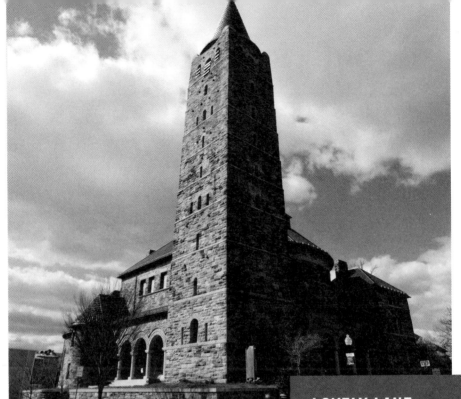

1884 Lovely Lane Methodist Church tower

It is yet one more in a long line of Baltimore firsts.

The beautiful Romanesque Revival structure on St. Paul Street dates to 1884; the original Lovely Lane chapel—or meeting house—was about two miles south of the current church, where there used to be a Lovely Lane but isn't anymore.

LOVELY LANE METHODIST CHURCH

WHAT: The mother church of American Methodism

WHERE: 2200 St. Paul St., Baltimore, Old Goucher

COST: Free

PRO TIP: The church houses and maintains a set of archives and a museum as well if the beauty of the building itself is not enough.

MARYLAND SCHOOL FOR THE BLIND

Where can you see a completely unique soccer game?

Finding a soccer game in full swing is no difficult task in the Baltimore area. Rec leagues, travel and club contests, pick-up games, middle and high school teams, and adult leagues (I play in one myself)—the opportunities to take in games are myriad.

Baltimore has been something of a soccer hotbed for decades: tiny University of Baltimore won a national championship in 1975; the Baltimore Bays were a mainstay of the old North American Soccer league; and when well-known international clubs come to play exhibitions at M&T Bank Stadium, a sellout is guaranteed.

But if you want to take in one of the more incredible and uplifting matches you're ever likely to see, head to the Maryland School for the Blind (MSB). In 2016, the school became the first in the nation to form a blind team. And a few years later, it became the location of the country's first youth blind soccer game, pitting the Maryland School for the Blind Bees against the Virginia School for the Blind Chiefs (for the record, the home squad pulled out a 2-1 victory).

The ball emits a jingle sound for location. The field is lined with boards to keep the ball in play. Other specific rules differentiate blind soccer from sighted soccer, but the sense of competition and camaraderie is precisely the same, if not heightened.

Several other soccer programs for the blind have been formed in the country, but MSB remains the epicenter for the sport, hosting the very first North American Blind Soccer Training Camp for both coaches and players in

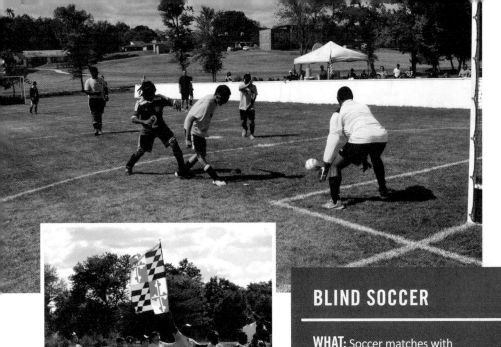

Blind soccer at the Maryland School for the Blind. Photos courtesy of Dotty Raynor

2018. The goal is to create a national team that can then ultimately compete in the Paralympics. So take in a game and—most likely—watch future Paralympians in the making.

MSB traces its roots to 1853, when it was in downtown Baltimore and was known as the Maryland Institution for the Instruction of the Blind.

MARYLAND SCIENCE CENTER OBSERVATORY

Can you really look directly at the sun?

The Maryland Science Center has been an Inner Harbor attraction for decades for visitors and city dwellers alike. In fact, the institution's founding actually stretches all the way back to 1797 when it was the Maryland Academy of Sciences. But the Science Center we all have come to know and love dates to 1976, with the arresting atrium lobby and popular IMAX theater arriving in 1986 and 1987, respectively. There's hardly a schoolkid anywhere in the metro area who hasn't been to the Maryland Science Center, and probably multiple times. But for free rooftop stargazing? That is something of a well-kept secret.

The deal is this: every Friday from 5:30 p.m. to 9:00 p.m., the Science Center opens up the

OBSERVATORY

WHAT: A free show of the night sky

WHERE: 601 Light St., Inner Harbor

COST: None for the telescope only; Science Center entrance fee is $19.95-$25.95, the IMAX is an additional fee

PRO TIP: The stargazing takes place outdoors and happens weather permitting, so dress appropriately. Also, it's best to give a call the day of to make sure it's still on: 410-545-2999.

Yes, it's free. But if you have paid for entrance to the museum, you can also observe the sun through the observatory's telescope on Friday and Saturday afternoons.

Back entrance of the Maryland Science Center

rooftop observatory for free public observations of the night sky, guided by knowledgeable staff. To check it out, head around the back of the building (in other words, pass by the main entrance facing the Harbor) to the group entrance door on Key Highway. Tell them what you're there for, and then enjoy the trip up to the roof and the Crosby Ramsey Memorial Observatory with its state-of-the-art telescope providing the dazzling show that is our corner of the cosmos.

HIS MASTER'S VOICE, WRIT LARGE

Where can you find an oversized replica of one of the most enduring logos in commercial history?

"Nipper" was the name of a 19th-century terrier mix owned by Mark Barraud, the brother of English artist Francis Barraud. When Mark died, Francis inherited Nipper, as well as a phonograph and recordings of Mark's voice that Mark had made. When Francis played the recordings, Nipper would cock his head and listen intently to "his master's voice." A painting was born.

Francis sold the painting to the Gramophone Company in 1899, which then adopted the image as a trademark for its American affiliate, the Victor Talking Machine Company (which would eventually become RCA Victor). That the logo is still instantly recognizable is a testament to its wonderful simplicity and effectiveness. Little Nipper still has legions of fans to this day, well more than a century after he was first committed to canvas; a brisk sale of Nipper collectibles is still in evidence on eBay.

What a treat then to gaze up and see "little" Nipper recreated in such gargantuan splendor! He stands (well, sits) 18 feet high and weighs more than 1,500 pounds. "How did

---

In operation since 1844, the Maryland Historical Society is a treasure chest, possessing more than 350,000 objects and seven million books and documents. It also has an online archive and allows researchers to access its documents by appointment.

Nipper in all his glory atop the Maryland Historical Society

NIPPER, THE RCA LOGO

WHAT: Oversized replica dog

WHERE: 201 W. Monument St., Mount Vernon

COST: Free to check out Nipper. Admission to the Historical Society is $6–$9.

PRO TIP: It goes without saying that the Historical Society itself is worth a visit, too. It's a terrific institution. But if for no other reason (even though there are many), they do sell replica Nippers inside.

he get there?" you might ask. Well, this particular Nipper began his life in the 1950s atop the roof of D&H Distributing Company, the local distributor for RCA. When D&H no longer wanted it, a collector bought the replica and displayed it at his house in Virginia. Eventually, it came back to Baltimore after the now-defunct City Life Museum purchased it. Nipper ultimately made his way to his current home atop the Maryland Historical Society, where he rarely fails to stop passersby and elicit smiles.

THE McKIM CENTER AND QUAKER FRIENDS MEETING HOUSE

Where is Baltimore's first free school building and oldest religious structure?

This is something of a two for one. In a city as old as Baltimore, concentrated historical sights are no huge surprise. But two lesser-known and less-celebrated sights are within close view of one another.

First, there is the McKim Center on Aisquith and Baltimore Streets. For 200 years, this building has served as a community resource center. It began life in 1821 as the first free school (a somewhat radical and very progressive notion at the time) in Baltimore and one of the first in the nation defiantly "open to all children, regardless of denomination or background." Still functioning as a community resource, to this day, the building has served as an outreach center, a night school, and a rec center.

The building itself was completed in 1835 and, as can be seen at first glance, was executed in a striking Greek Doric design. It got its inspiration from the monumental gateway to the

---

OLD, HISTORICAL BUILDINGS IN JONESTOWN

WHAT: Two disparate historical sites sharing a block

WHERE: The McKim Center: 1120 E. Baltimore St.; Friends Meeting House: 1201 E. Fayette St., Jonestown

COST: Free

PRO TIP: Just one block to the south of McKim on Lloyd Street is the Jewish Museum of Maryland and the adjacent Lloyd Street Synagogue. Built in 1845, it was Maryland's first synagogue and the nation's third oldest.

1821 McKim Center

1781 Quaker Friends Meeting House

Acropolis as well as from a temple in the Agora of Athens that still stands to this day.

Behind the McKim Center, about 100 yards away on Aisquith just before Fayette, is the Quaker Friends Meeting House. It's a striking building primarily for its simplicity and age. Dating to 1781, it's a plain two-story brick house designed for practicing Quakers and remains the city's oldest religious-use structure. Not only did the McKim family worship here; so did city patron Johns Hopkins and the first president of the B&O Railroad, Philip E. Thomas. Ultimately, Quaker influence grew in Baltimore and continues today, evidenced perhaps most conspicuously by the lovely Friends School campus, established in 1784, as the signs tell you, in Roland Park.

What goes on at the McKim Center these days? In the center's words: "Determination. Courage. Teamwork. Mutual support. Joy. Triumph. Success. And the building of strong community." That's just as it's been for 200 years.

MEMORIAL STADIUM

Where can you channel the glory days of Baltimore sports?

As far as the sporting world goes, the late 1960s to early '70s were a glorious time in Baltimore. In one seven-year period, the Orioles appeared in the World Series four times, winning two of them, while the Colts appeared in three championships/Super Bowls, winning twice and giving the city concurrent champions in both baseball and football. Incredibly, that same season saw the Baltimore Bullets of the NBA make the championship finals, too. Alas, the Milwaukee Bucks and some fella later known as Kareem Abdul-Jabbar ruined that potential trifecta.

Apart from this smashing success, what the Colts and Orioles had in common in those days was Memorial Stadium, that venerable old place on 33rd Street. It's long gone now, of course—the O's moving to Major League Baseball's best stadium at Camden Yards, the Colts off to Indianapolis, and the Ravens taking up residence in their terrific stadium across the street from the Orioles.

So what's in the old Memorial Stadium's place now? Fittingly, a baseball diamond. There's a YMCA and new senior housing there now, too, but the streets are situated just the

---

Memorial Stadium witnessed the Orioles winning the World Series in 1966 (4–0 over the LA Dodgers) and 1970 (4–1 over Cincinnati), as well as the 1959 Colts winning the NFL championship. Four other championships (3 for the Colts and 1 more for the O's) took place elsewhere.

Memorial Stadium home plate

33RD STREET (EVERYONE KNOWS THAT ADDRESS)

WHAT: Site of the old Memorial Stadium

WHERE: 900 E. 33rd St., Waverly

COST: Free

PRO TIP: Portions of the old Memorial Stadium façade as well as other artifacts can be seen at Camden Yards, where the Orioles have played since 1992.

same as they were when you took them to get to a game at the stadium. Even better, the white houses along 36th Street still stand, and you can imagine why batters used to complain about how the white baseball got lost to sight against those houses on the way from pitcher to home plate.

Speaking of home plate, the YMCA's field has its home plate in exactly the same spot where Memorial Stadium's used to be. Cool.

MISS CARTER'S KITCHEN

Could it have been the pudding?

In 2019, the Ravens and their sensation of a quarterback, the precocious Lamar Jackson, had one of the greatest regular seasons in league history (alas, an early playoff exit overshadowed the 14-2, No.1-seed regular season campaign). Jackson, the league MVP and Pro Bowl MVP that year, seemed to break another record every week.

Along the way, Jackson became the youngest First Team All-Pro quarterback in league history. His five 100-yard rushing games were the most ever by a 22-year-old quarterback. His 36 passing touchdowns were the most in a single season for a quarterback under 23. Jackson was also the youngest quarterback in league history to post two perfect passer ratings in one season; his season passer rating was also a record high for his age.

Beyond these age-related records, his 1,206 rushing yards were the most for any quarterback, at any age, in NFL history. Likewise, he was the only player to rush for 1,000 yards and pass for 30 touchdowns in the same season and the only quarterback with 3,000-plus passing yards and 1,000-plus rushing yards in the same season. And despite the playoff loss, Jackson became

---

It's not just pudding at Miss Carter's Kitchen. Jackson and his Ravens teammates were also apparently enamored with the pasta, steak and shrimp, wings, collard greens, and mac & cheese.

Lamar Jackson's favorite

BANANA PUDDING

WHAT: A Lamar Jackson favorite

WHERE: 2804 Edmondson Ave., Mosher/Western

COST: The banana pudding is $4.99.

PRO TIP: Miss Carter's has another location as well, perfect for the downtown worker set, at 218 North Liberty Street.

the first player to compile 350-plus passing yards and 100-plus rushing yards during that game.

So to what do we attribute all this? Well, freakish athletic abilities, of course—plus hard work, intelligence, perseverance, and great coaches and teammates. But maybe it was also the banana pudding at Miss Carter's Kitchen. Jackson, as well as several of his Ravens teammates, often showed up at this soul food spot in West Baltimore pining for the stuff. As a result, maybe this is a secret no more. "I think now, with all the exposure, I'm going to have to keep banana pudding on the menu," said owner Cia Carter.

"THE MOST DANGEROUS OF ALL ALLIED SPIES"

Where did one of the 20th century's most decorated Americans get her start?

The list of accolades is so extraordinary as to be almost unbelievable. That they were bestowed upon a woman in an era of extreme gender inequality makes the story even more amazing.

Many people had not heard of Virginia Hall before author Sonia Purnell's 2019 book, *A Woman of No Importance: The Untold Story of the American Spy Who Helped Win World War II*. Purnell's biography has a title that might seem hyperbolic to some. But a review of Hall's extraordinary life and service will dispel any notions of exaggeration. By the end of her career, Hall had been awarded the American Distinguished Service Cross (the second-highest Army military award and the only instance of a woman being awarded one during all of WWII), the French Croix de Guerre, and the British MBE (Most Excellent Order of the British Empire) for her role in bringing down the Nazis through her spycraft. Her work allegedly earned her not only Nazi spite but also begrudging respect as she was, in their view, "the most dangerous of all Allied spies."

VIRGINIA HALL, SPY

WHAT: Alma mater of an extraordinary and underappreciated woman

WHERE: Roland Park Country School, 5204 Roland Ave., Roland Park

COST: Free

PRO TIP: Hall's family eventually moved to Parkton, in Baltimore County. A historical marker indicates the homestead and can be viewed on York Road (MD 45) north of Stablers Church Road.

Roland Park Country School, alma mater of Virginia Hall

Hall spent her childhood and adolescence in Baltimore, living with her family in Reservoir Hill and Tuscany-Canterbury. She attended Baltimore's Roland Park Country School (as did other famous alums such as poet Adrienne Rich and actress Julie Bowen). For a glimpse of the life she would lead, you need only look at the dedication of her 1924 yearbook class page, still on file at the school: "She is, by her own confession, cantankerous and capricious, but in spite of it all we would not do without her; for she is our class-president, the editor-in-chief of this book, and one of the mainstays of the basket-ball and hockey teams. She has been acclaimed the most original of our class, and she lives up to her reputation at all times. The one thing to expect from [Hall] is the unexpected."

A Woman of No Importance, the film about Virginia Hall, is in production from Paramount and stars Daisy Ridley.

THE NAME REMAINS THE SAME . . .

Where will you find the only street name still in use that was part of the city's original plan?

If 18th-century structures get you excited, there are plenty of those in Baltimore (and a few highlighted in this book). Explore Federal Hill or Fells Point; those neighborhoods are full of buildings from the 1700s. You can also head to Jonestown/Old Town to see where Baltimore got its start, way back in 1661 when the Englishman David Jones built his house on the banks of a stream that would later be given his name.

But to see the oldest developed corner of the city, head instead to the intersection of Baltimore and North Calvert Streets. Calvert was the name given this street in 1729, and it has remained the same for almost 300 years, the only such street in the original city plan with that distinction.

True, this intersection doesn't currently retain any 18th-century buildings, but that does not mean there are no lovely or historic structures. For example, what is today the Alexander Brown Restaurant, at 135 East Baltimore, is, of course, the former headquarters of Alex. Brown, Inc., which was the country's very first investment bank, founded in 1800. The two-story brick building you see today was constructed in 1901 and is one of the very few area buildings to have survived the Great Fire of 1904. The building's survival was due to the

---

If you look closely, you can still spot the scars from the Great Fire on the large metal front doors of the Alex. Brown building.

Alex. Brown building

Everything has changed in a few hundred years, except the street names.

brick and granite construction materials. It also happens to have been the first building in the country to be heated entirely by electricity.

CALVERT & BALTIMORE

WHAT: Original intersection from Baltimore's earliest days

WHERE: E. Baltimore and N. Calvert Sts., downtown

COST: Free

PRO TIP: Just one block to the north, at Calvert and Fayette, stands the Battle Monument, commemorating those who died defending Baltimore from the British in the War of 1812; its construction began in 1815. It's a beautiful monument, but also historically significant: This was the country's first public monument, and it is believed to be the world's first memorial erected to the everyday soldier (as opposed to officers and other elites).

NATURALIZATION

Where in Baltimore do immigrants become US citizens?

It's difficult these days to discuss immigration and not invite a heated, partisan argument. The best way to get past all that is to watch a naturalization service. At 101 West Lombard Street, in the offices of the United States District Court, District of Maryland, immigrants from around the world take the oath of allegiance, a process that has remained little changed since 1790.

It's an uplifting and heartwarming ceremony, and the diversity on display is staggering. In a typical ceremony, anywhere from 20 to 40 applicants, hailing from dozens of nations, are sworn in as new citizens of the United States. It's a process that takes place behind closed doors and usually witnessed only by family members. But bearing witness to one reminds us that lost in those heated arguments about immigration are actual human beings, obtaining a thing of inestimable value that many of us rarely think twice about.

Baltimore is a natural location for such ceremonies as the city has been a landing point for immigrants since its founding almost 300 years ago. Indeed, for a stretch of decades spanning the 19th and 20th centuries, Baltimore was second only to New

IMMIGRATION AND NATURALIZATION

WHAT: Where immigrants become US citizens

WHERE: 101 W. Lombard St., Downtown

COST: Free

PRO TIP: To find out when a ceremony is taking place, visit www.mdd.uscourts.gov ceremony-dates. Additionally, this is a courthouse; so be prepared for standard security measures.

United States District Court, District of Maryland

York in processing immigrants to this county, as many as 40,000 per year. The numbers are much smaller today, of course, but no less worth witnessing.

Newly arrived immigrants used to come to Baltimore at Fells Point's Broadway Pier, a location instantly recognizable to fans of the NBC series, *Homicide: Life on the Street.*

NUT AND BOLT

Did these fall from a giant's toolbox?

Mount Royal Elementary/Middle School occupies a particularly artsy spot, at 121 McMechen Street in Bolton Hill. That puts the school squarely in the heart of the expanding Maryland Institute College of Art (MICA) campus. MICA has been around since 1826, making it one of the country's oldest art schools—one increasingly recognized as ranking among the best.

Mount Royal Elementary/Middle can claim some illustrious history of its own. Since its opening in 1958, it has been desegregated, making it one of the first such schools of its kind in the city. These days, a robust arts curriculum contributes to Mount Royal's uniqueness. Indeed, the school routinely employs interns from MICA to help infuse arts instruction across content areas, wisely recognizing the impact of artistic expression on the growth of young students' intellectual abilities.

So it's no surprise then that Mount Royal's campus is home to one of the more delightfully quirky public arts installations in the city—one that people other than students, staff, and associated parents rarely see.

Nut and Bolt is a steel sculpture gracing the outside of a walkway that runs between wings of the school. It takes the shape of a huge gray wrench tightened around a brightly

---

Nut and Bolt was created by J. Arthur Benson, who headed up MICA's sculpture department for more than 30 years.

Nut and Bolt, *at Mount Royal Elementary/ Middle School*

painted nut, and appears to be aiding in holding up the walkway.

It's easy to walk right by and take no notice; but if you look up and take it in, it's likely that you will feel just a bit of joy. And what better place to feel such a sentiment than at an institution actively shaping our future leaders?

NUT AND BOLT SCULPTURE

WHAT: Public art

WHERE: 121 McMechen St., Bolton Hill

COST: Free

PRO TIP: While folks shouldn't really be skulking around public schools, generally speaking, the raised *Nut and Bolt* sculpture creates a causeway under which it is perfectly natural to pass, as it connects McMechen and Mosher Streets.

NUTSHELL STUDIES OF UNEXPLAINED DEATH

Which is more striking: the utility or the artistry?

Many people would call it a tie. First, the utility: the nutshell studies of unexplained death are extraordinary objects. They date to a time before the field of forensic science was even invented. In the early decades of the 20th century, medical examiners and crime-scene "investigators" had no organized training. Into this void stepped Mrs. Frances Glessner Lee, a wealthy socialite who, in 1931, helped found and fund the Department of Legal Medicine at Harvard.

But beyond the money, Mrs. Lee's larger contribution was in her nutshell dioramas, 18 in total, which she created herself. These are incredible miniaturized crime-scene reproductions that police, coroners, and forensic examiners could study using magnifying glasses and flashlights, while poring over the meticulous detail in a search for clues that might help solve a crime—in her words, help police "convict the guilty, clear the innocent, and find the truth in a nutshell."

Not only did each diorama contain a corpse and the gruesome details of a hideous murder, but every item was carefully planned and could be a clue. Literally nothing was superfluous: flowers, boxes of chocolates, silverware, and more. The angles of bullet holes and blood spatters, too, were created with precision and intention.

Lee reportedly spent upwards of $7,000 on average creating each diorama, an amount roughly equivalent to the cost of a new home at the time.

Nutshell diorama. Photo courtesy of the Renwick Gallery

NUTSHELL CRIME STUDIES

WHAT: Forensics training in miniature

WHERE: Office of the Chief Medical Examiner, 900 W. Baltimore St., Poppleton

COST: Free

PRO TIP: A change in policy as of 2020 means the nutshell studies are no longer open to public visits; however, potential future public exhibits are possible. Images of the studies can be found in various locations online.

After Lee died in 1962, the models became the property of the Maryland Medical Examiner's office, and where they are *still* used in training.

As for the art, these are amazing pieces, striking in their extreme attention to the most miniscule detail and remarkable for the use of features such as working light switches and door handles, knitted fabrics for clothing, real lead in tiny pencils, and real tobacco in stray cigarettes. Her scenes, each a macabre dollhouse, were based on actual crimes she reconstructed through the use of police reports and witness statements.

OLD ST. PAUL'S

Is less than 170 years old *really* all that old?

The church that currently occupies the spot at 233 North Charles Street is *pretty* old, dating to 1854. But in Baltimore, which predates the formation of the United States, being barely pre-Civil War doesn't qualify a structure as being all that ancient. So then, why is St. Paul's Episcopal Church more commonly known around these parts as "Old" St. Paul's?

Well, if we keep going back in time, there was another St. Paul's church here before this one, built in 1812–14. (It burned and was eventually replaced by the current structure). So now we're stretching back some 200 years. Even in a city as old as Baltimore, founded in 1729, that's not bad. But to go back even further: it was in that year, 1729, that the church set up shop in its current location, culminating in the eventual 1812–14 building. So now we're approaching three hundred years in this

---

A half block to the south, at the intersection with Lexington, is the lovely Romanesque Revival flatiron Fidelity & Deposit Company building. This 1890s building was one of the few in the immediate area to survive the Great Fire of 1904. Stand across the street to pick out an amazing sight: if you look closely, you can spot the façade of the original 19th-century building's eight floors. But between 1912 and 1915, workers built around the existing façade and expanded the building by seven stories, almost perfectly incorporating all the design elements of the original.

Old St. Paul's Church on Charles Street

OLD ST. PAUL'S CHURCH

WHAT: 17th-century religious affiliations

WHERE: 233 N. Charles St., Downtown

COST: Free

PRO TIP: One mile to the west, at Redwood Street and Martin Luther King, Jr. Boulevard, is the 1799 Old St. Paul's Cemetery. Among the notables buried there are George Armistead, Declaration of Independence signer Samuel Chase, John Eager Howard, and, for a time, Francis Scott Key, whose remains were later relocated.

same spot. Not bad. But how about we keep moving further, back into the mists of time, to an era predating Baltimore by several more decades? That is when, in 1692, the colonial General Assembly, under the Establishment Act, created thirty parishes of the Church of England (better known to us now as the Anglican Church, whose adherents in the United States are known as Episcopalians, thus the name of this church . . .) in the colony of Maryland. Today's "Old St. Paul's," a still-functioning and vigorous Episcopal congregation, stretches its roots to that time, predating the establishment of the country itself by more than eighty years. Okay, so that's pretty old.

OPEN DOORS

Have an interest in gaining entry to places otherwise off-limits?

Doors Open Baltimore—dubbed "the city's largest festival of architecture and neighborhoods"—began in 2014 and just seems to keep getting better and better. While Doors Open is really no secret, I include it here because its attractions are for sites that are the very definition of hidden gems and are available for viewing only very occasionally, if not as one-offs. In short, look at Doors Open as something of a citywide open house.

Every year in the fall, selected sites are opened to the public and are available for viewing and informative talks led by designers, architects, historians, and other experts in various fields. The carefully selected sites, rotating every year (with some fan favorites repeating, such as the American Brewery Building, at 1701 North Gay Street), are generally clustered by neighborhood, so it's easy to take in multiple sites with little effort. Likewise, the entire operation is self-guided, so you can pick and choose what you'd like to see and how to get there. Once you've arrived at your destination, you can take advantage of the on-site expert to give you the inside scoop.

Baltimore is blessed with a wealth of iconic and fascinating buildings. Countless times, I have passed by one or another

---

THE ANNUAL DOORS OPEN BALTIMORE

WHAT: Entry into loads of otherwise restricted locations

WHERE: Locations vary. For info: www.doorsopenbaltimore.org

COST: Free

PRO TIP: Virtually every site is accessible by public transport.

American Brewery Building, one of the favorite stops in the Doors Open Baltimore annual event

and wondered what it was like inside. Invariably, at least one such building winds up on the Doors Open itinerary every year. It's like scratching a longtime itch. And, yes, it really is free—just one more reason this is a charming city.

Doors Open gladly accepts volunteers, though some training is required. For info: www. doorsopenbaltimore.org/volunteer.

ORPHEUS SCOTT KEY

Who exactly is that colossus lurking over the grounds of hallowed Fort McHenry?

That huge statue looming over the grounds at Fort McHenry is indeed dedicated to Francis Scott Key, but is that McHenry, clutching a lyre and completely nude apart from headband and carefully placed fig leaf? Well, no.

The statue is of Orpheus, the legendary poet and musician of Greek mythology. In 1914, Congress appropriated funds for a monument to celebrate the 100-year anniversary of the writing of "The Star-Spangled Banner." Sculptor Charles H. Niehaus, working in allegory, created *Orpheus with the Awkward Foot* to represent Francis Scott Key. So, no, that huge nude (24 feet in height, standing atop 15 feet of pedestal and base—at the time, the largest cast bronze statue in the world) is not Key. But by looking more closely, you'll eventually find Key's likeness—just don't look upward. Instead, check out the medallion near the base. There you will find the man himself, in profile, with birth and death dates.

One contemporary critic wrote: "It is most gratifying to note that the sculptor has had the courage to make a symbolical figure and thus to honor the sublime art of music. Thus he has given us an Orpheus instead of presenting the world with one more unlovely portrait of mere man."

At the dedication of the Orpheus monument in 1922, Warren Harding became the first president to be broadcast on radio coast to coast, lauding Baltimore as "the one great Atlantic port over which no enemy flag has ever flown."

Francis Scott Key Memorial on the grounds of Fort McHenry, birthplace of the Star-Spangled Banner

F.S. KEY STATUE (BUT NOT OF KEY)

WHAT: *Orpheus* sculpture

WHERE: Fort McHenry National Monument and Historic Shrine, 2400 E. Fort Ave.

COST: $15 for ages 16 and up; free for ages 15 and under. The grounds, where Orpheus stands, are free to walk.

PRO TIP: Every morning at 10 a.m., the standard 50-star flag is lowered and replaced with the replica 15-star garrison flag, and then done again in reverse at 5 p.m. During these ceremonies, visitors gather around and aid in folding the massive standard so that it does not touch the ground. It's one seriously cool way to be part of history—and the present.

But not everyone was thrilled with the winning design. Many, notably sculptors whose designs were not picked, expressed piqued astonishment that a statue to Key didn't, well, depict Key. Nevertheless, Orpheus was chosen.

THE OTTOBAR

One of the 10 best live music venues in America is in Baltimore?

Yes, indeed, according to no less an authority than *Rolling Stone* Magazine, which included the Ottobar on its esteemed list in 2018, alongside such legends as the Hollywood Bowl and Red Rocks. The magazine extolled the virtues of this "dingy-yet-beloved rock club [that] has hosted all kinds of bands—including improbably massive ones like the White Stripes and the Yeah Yeah Yeahs."

The place has cachet, credentials, and history, and thus routinely attracts not only nationally known bands but locals gone big, such as Animal Collective and Beach House, who know where to come when they want a more intimate experience than the national arena tour. (And like many local in-spots, it's not uncommon to spot John Waters prowling about.)

The Ottobar has been around since 1997, but its move to North Howard Street in 2001, long before the area began to see revitalization and gentrification, made it something of a little-known pilgrimage site, reserved for those in the know. But a place this good can't stay a secret for long. It's often the case that if you ask locals if they know of the Ottobar, they will say, "Yes, absolutely." But ask again where it is, and well . . . in other words, get there before too many people know more than they

THE OTTOBAR

WHAT: Intimate and very well-respected music club

WHERE: 2549 N. Howard St., Remington

COST: Ticket prices vary by act but are surprisingly reasonable.

PRO TIP: The Ottobar can be visited seven nights a week in the upstairs bar. In other words, it's open outside of show times.

The Ottobar in Remington

know, and this little, still somewhat-secret gem gets harder and harder to get in to.

As *Rolling Stone* aptly put it, "Ottobar offers much more than consistent live music. It's become an important community pillar, a home base and an undeniable hidden gem of the I-95 tour circuit."

Like any good club, the Ottobar offers tasteful merch: clothes, stickers, phone cases, and more.

OUIJA BOARD 7-11

Seriously? The Ouija board was created here?

The Baltimorean Elijah Bond was an inventor who had multiple patents to his name before he died in 1921. His most famous invention is the Ouija board, that multi-million unit seller that still captivates to this day, more than 130 years since its creation.

The legend runs thus: in 1890, at what is now a 7-11 on the corner of Charles and Centre, stood a boarding house called Langham Hotel. And in that house, Bond; Charles Kennard, the first manufacturer of the Ouija board; and medium Helen Peters were participating in a séance. Kemmard explained the event: "I remarked that we had not yet settled upon a name, and as the board had helped us in other ways, we would ask it to propose one. It spelled out O-U-I-J-A. When I asked the meaning of the word it said 'good luck.' Miss Peters there upon withdrew from her neck a chain which had at the end a locket, on it the figure of a woman and at the top the word 'Ouija.' We asked her if she thought of this name and she said she had not."

You are, of course, not required to believe this tale, nor have any interest in Ouija at all. But you have to admit: it's totally bizarre and kind of cool that the famous game was named here—in what is now a convenience store. The plaque commemorating the event is hung just inside the door.

Depending on the source, Ouija is called the best-selling board game of all time or ranked second to Monopoly.

The old Langham Hotel in Mount Vernon, where the Ouija board was born

7-11 CONVENIENCE STORE WITH AN EERIE HISTORY

WHAT: Where the Ouija board was created

WHERE: 529 N. Charles St., Mount Vernon

COST: Free

PRO TIP: Of course, if you are a Ouija aficionado, your next stop should be about 10 blocks to the northwest, at Greenmount Cemetery, where Bond is buried. Even in this graveyard where many notables, including John Wilkes Booth, are buried, you can't miss Bond's gravesite: his is the gravestone with the Ouija board carved into one side.

YES **OUIJA** NO
WAS NAMED HERE

History is rife with tales of prophecy, fortune-telling, and divination. At this site in April 1890, one of the world's most popular methods for divining one's fate received its name, and the Ouija board — Baltimore's famous Mystifying Oracle" — was born.

For generations, Ouija's mysterious messages have intrigued people of all ages. When users rest their fingertips lightly on the planchette, the pointer moves over the board's alphabet to spell out words, answer questions, and deliver cryptic messages. Ever fascinating, Ouija has become an integral part of popular American culture.

It was here at 529 North Charles Street where the famous Ouija board received its name. According to those present, the board named itself when asked what it wanted to be called.

On that night an American icon was created — one that every generation revisits. Led by William Fuld, Ouija became a leading industry in Baltimore, produced in thirteen different factories across the city from 1890 to 1966.

In 1919, Ouija's first manufacturer, Charles Kennard, recounted the origins of Ouija's name to the *Baltimore American* and *Sun* papers:

One evening about April 1890, while trying the board with a Miss Peters... in a large boarding house at that time on the corner of Charles and Center streets... I remarked that we had not yet settled upon a name, and as the board had helped us in other ways, we would ask it to propose one. It spelled out O-U-I-J-A. When I asked the meaning of the word it said 'good luck.' Miss Peters there upon withdrew from her neck a chain which had at the end a locket, on it the figure of a woman and at the top the word 'Ouija.' We asked her if she had thought of this name, and she said she had not. We then adopted the word."

— Charles W. Kennard, First to Manufacture the Ouija Board

 Stephanie Rawlings-Blake
Mayor, City of Baltimore

 Talking Board Historical Society
Sponsor

Baltimore National Heritage Area

Ouija and Mystifying Oracle are registered trademarks of Hasbro, Inc.

Commemorative Ouija marker, inside the 7-11 where the Langham once stood

EXCUSE MY DUST

What does Dorothy Parker have to do with the NAACP?

Writer and satirist Dorothy Parker desired an early demise. She attempted suicide, unsuccessfully, four times before dying of natural causes at age 73. On the occasion of her 70th birthday, she quipped, "If I had any decency, I'd be dead. All my friends are." Those friends included some of the most celebrated writers and artists of her day, F. Scott Fitzgerald, Dashiell Hammett, and Ernest Hemingway among them.

When she died, she left her estate to Martin Luther King Jr., whom she had never met but admired. When he was assassinated a year later, the estate became the property of the NAACP. But Parker's friend, playwright Lillian Hellman, executor of Parker's estate, bitterly contested the arrangement, furious that the prodigious royalties of Parker's estate did not go to her.

After Parker's cremation, Hellman neglected to pick up Parker's ashes. So they were eventually sent to Parker's lawyer's office, where they sat for 15 years. When news of this made the papers, the NAACP stepped in and took possession—and to this day, receives royalties on Parker's works.

And so that is why Dorothy Parker's ashes sit in a memorial garden in northwest Baltimore, home to the NAACP's national

DOROTHY PARKER MEMORIAL

WHAT: Parker's ashes

WHERE: 4805 Mt. Hope Dr., Lochearn

COST: Free

PRO TIP: As of this writing, the NAACP, after a move downtown to Wells Fargo Center, is considering another move to Washington, DC in 2021 or 2022. No word on how or when or if Parker's ashes will move as well.

NAACP national headquarters before the organization's move to downtown

Plaque marking the remains of writer Dorothy Parker

headquarters. The dedication plaque is lovely, paying homage to Parker's "noble spirit which celebrated the oneness of humankind and to the bonds of everlasting friendship between Black and Jewish people." And true to Parker's wit, it also includes her suggested epitaph: "Excuse my dust."

The circular design of the tablet atop Parker's ashes was a nod to her being a founding member of the Algonquin Round Table, the collection of New York writers and artists who thrived in the 1920s.

POOL NO. 2

Why do those ladders lead to dirt?

Baltimore has a tortured history with segregation and integration. The city officially began integration years before *Brown v. the Board of Education* and saw civil rights protests much earlier than many other major cities. But in some very real and visible respects, segregation continues in much of the city, a legacy of redlining and other historical initiatives designed to keep the races separate and wealth concentrated in the hands of whites at the expense of nonwhites.

For the first half of the 20th century, city parks were still segregated, so Druid Hill Park had a separate "Negro Section," an area with tennis courts, a playground, and "Pool No. 2." While six city-run pools, including nearby Pool No. 1, catered to whites, Pool No. 2 was the only one for the city's hundreds of

---

Writing about a 1948 integrated tennis match at Druid Hill, where Blacks and whites played together in protest and subsequently got roughed up by the cops, the great H. L. Mencken wrote: "The public parks are supported by the taxpayer, including the colored taxpayer, for the health and pleasure of the whole people. Why should cops be sent into them to separate those people against their will into separate herds? Why should the law set up distinctions and discriminations which the persons directly affected themselves reject?" By 1956, all the city parks, including Druid Hill and its pools, were fully integrated.

The once-segregated Pool No. 2 in Druid Hill Park

DRUID HILL OLD POOL

WHAT: A once-segregated pool, now powerful open-air art

WHERE: Shop and Commissary Rds., Druid Hill Park

COST: Free

PRO TIP: The Druid Hill Park pool still operates today, with a standard summer season. It's a bargain at $2 per-person admission. It's located just north of the northeastern side of the lake, off East Drive.

thousands of African American residents. The pool, 105 feet by 100 feet—with a paltry deep end of only seven-and-a-half feet—saw between 600 and 1,200 visitors a day during the summer. Originally constructed more than 100 years ago, the pool still stands today, but in the form of public, haunting, and little-known art. The pool itself is filled with dirt and covered in grass, while the pool's apparatuses—lifeguard chairs, ladders, diving board scaffolding—remain, painted in bright blue. Ringing the site are artworks in paint and tile, executed in the 1990s by local artist Joyce J. Scott. The bathhouses are also still standing.

PSYCHEDELIC, MAN

Where can you find a mural inspired by a key figure in Woodstock lore?

It's been more than half a century since Woodstock, a touchstone moment in the history of the counterculture. That August 1969 event would be followed just four months later by the attempted West Coast reprise at Altamont Raceway, and the ensuing drug-fueled madness, complete with homicide, became shorthand for all that went wrong with the dreams of the peace-and-love generation. With it, the sixties ended, both figuratively and literally.

But Woodstock retains its sacred place in pop culture for its three days of fun, music, peace, and love. There are many enduring images from that vaunted concert, and one of them is the famous "Light" VW bus, painted by Baltimorean Dr. Bob Hieronimus. In his words, "a rolling billboard of symbols [that] would reach people with their messages without ever needing words," spreading the message of the Age of Aquarius "when humanity will be aligned with the divine plan through cosmic vibration." That bus, completely covered with psychedelia, was photographed by *Rolling Stone* and the Associated Press and became a symbol of all that Woodstock stood for.

Another Dr. Bob creation—not quite so psychedelic but certainly retaining some of those same qualities—graces the

HIERONIMUS ART

WHAT: Public mural

WHERE: W. 36th St. and Roland Ave., Hampden

COST: Free

PRO TIP: On the bottom right of the mural, look for the artist's homage to the Hampden Trolley Line, in 1885 the nation's first trolley line, which used to service the neighborhood.

Dr. Bob Hieronimus-inspired mural in Hampden

1882 Hampden Hall, at the corner of West 36th Street and Roland Avenue. This mural was painted back in 1975 in preparation for the then-coming bicentennial; along with the 13-star American flag, the mural honors the neighborhood's two WWII Congressional Medal of Honor recipients.

Dr. Bob is the founder and still host of 21st Century Radio, a show "focused on Consciousness, Paranormal, UFOs, Conspiracies, American Symbols and Symbology, Cryptozoology, Energy News, Magic, Environment, Food Safety, Health, History Rewritten, Art, Mystic and Occult, Planetary Research, Religious Studies, Science News, and so much more!"

PUSHPIN BUS SHELTER

What would it look like if a giant Google Maps pushpin fell from the sky and impaled a bus stop?

Waiting for the bus is rarely fun. But when your wait puts you in close proximity to oversized art, it becomes much more tolerable. This is the case at Highland Avenue and Baltimore Street. There, the bus stop features a giant red pushpin, standing some 17 feet tall, impaling the shelter's roof. It calls to mind those "You Are Here" map graphics with your location denoted by a pushpin.

In this case, "You Are Here" is the title of the art, only the phrase is in Spanish—*Estamos Aqui*—and the letters ride across the top of shelter's roof as if in a wave. The Spanish reflects the diversity of the surrounding neighborhood, where waves of mostly Central American immigrants have made their homes in recent years. Servicing four MTA routes, this is one of the most-used stops in the city. The sculpture came about courtesy of local grants—including $25,000 from the PNC Bank Transformative Art Prize—and was a collaboration between artists in the Highlandtown Arts District and officials from the Southeast Community Development Corporation.

As for the art itself, the pin is actually an upside-down light pole, set at an angle as if it has been thrown from a

---

As for those waves of Central American immigrants: Lucky for us, many of them have brought their culinary traditions with them and have opened up local eateries not only in this neighborhood, Baltimore Highlands, but also nearby in Highlandtown and Upper Fells Point.

"You Are Here" East Baltimore bus stop

distance and then speared into the shelter's roof. The top of the pin, in stark attention-grabbing red, was constructed from synthetic stucco.

Here you are. Enjoy it.

BUS STOP

WHAT: Bus stop as public art

WHERE: N. Highland Ave. at Baltimore St., Baltimore Highlands

COST: Free

PRO TIP: A little over a mile to the southeast is Greektown. Unlike so many other once-ethnic enclaves where successive generations decamped, Greeks still predominate here, from the shops and restaurants to the denizens on their stoops.

PYRAMIDS ON THE PATAPSCO

What exactly are those things?

Artist Jim Sanborn may not be a household name for most Americans, but his list of accomplishments in the arts is extremely impressive. His works have been or are currently on display all across the United States, as well as in Europe and Asia. But back in 1977, his first commissioned public sculpture was the Patapsco River Project, in Baltimore's Middle Branch Park where it meets Cherry Hill Park.

The Patapsco River Project, extending almost 100 feet across, calls to mind Egyptian temples, and that is not by accident. Inspired by Sanborn's interest in Mayan architecture as well as a trip to Egypt to see the pyramids, the concrete-based structures taper upward to steel rust-colored tops. The central room is flanked by five pyramids on either side and contains a reflection pool that receives direct sunlight.

Community and corporate involvement in the project made its installation a reality: Bethlehem Steel donated the steel, city workers poured and mixed the concrete, and a private local company sheathed the metal. When it was completed over four decades ago, it was a beautiful piece. Alas, a lack of maintenance resulted in a weed-choked,

---

The Patapsco River Project was originally part of the 1977 Baltimore Sculpture Symposium. Of the four original pieces erected in the city, only one other is still around: the Atlantic Blue Roller Column on Russell Street.

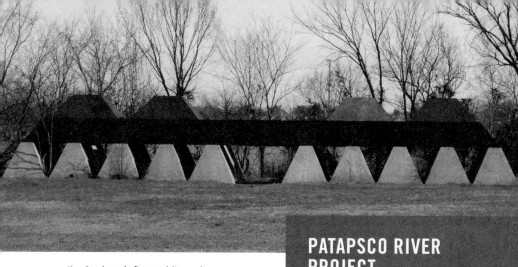

Jim Sanborn's first public sculpture

PATAPSCO RIVER PROJECT

WHAT: Public art

WHERE: Grassy space between S. Hanover St., Potee St., and Reedbird Ave., just to the west of the Patapsco River and south of Med Star Hospital, Cherry Hill

COST: Free

PRO TIP: Middle Branch Park continues to get love, with major restoration/development/improvement plans in place for 2020 and beyond, helping to elevate a beautiful but currently underappreciated waterfront space.

rusted, and graffitied hulk that assured that the few people who stumbled across it couldn't tell what it was or be aware of the creator's international prominence.

Happily, in 2019, Visit Baltimore and Baltimore's Office of Promotion & the Arts spearheaded a cleanup of the monument. It is again prominent and well worth a visit. But that's only a first step. The Patapsco River Project could use a little more love—and plenty more visitors.

ROLAND PARK PATHS

Sledding your way through a neighborhood?

The North Baltimore neighborhood of Roland Park, developed between 1890 and 1920, was the country's first planned community. Its lead architects adhered to the principles of the City Beautiful Movement, which emphasized working with the natural landscape instead of plowing through it. Neighborhood levies went toward beautification projects and upkeep.

It was, at the time, a novel concept. Roland Park was originally conceived of as a streetcar suburb (post-annexation in 1918, it lost its "suburban" moniker but not its suburban feel), allowing residents to enjoy the cooler countryside while easily accessing the streetcar to downtown. The addition of the nation's first strip mall (see page 44) made "country" living even easier, as now residents could obtain goods without leaving their leafy neighborhood.

In the construction of Roland Park, Frederick Law Olmstead (responsible for Baltimore's Druid Hill Park and New York's Central Park, among others) created 18 footpaths, allowing residents to easily navigate their neighborhood in places where the rolling, curvy landscape did not allow for automobiles. Even with today's ubiquitous auto traffic, the paths remain, giving Roland Parkers an almost magical method of traverse. Each path is named—Sunset Path, for example, because it gives a view of the sun setting over Cylburn Arboretum, around a mile

Today's Roland Park has lost none of its charm or beauty. It's no wonder that the neighborhood is still studied and cited in urban-planning textbooks and classrooms.

Laurel Path in Roland Park

NEIGHBORHOOD
TRAVERSES

WHAT: Hidden pathways through Roland Park

WHERE: Locations vary, Roland Park

COST: Free

PRO TIP: A map of the Roland Park pathways can be downloaded here: rolandpark.org/wp-content/uploads/2016/05/RPFootpaths.pdf.

to the west. The other paths are Audley End, Brier, Climbing, Hepburn, Hilltop, Kittery, Laurel, Litchfield, Rye, Shipton, Squirrel, St. Margaret's, Ten Oaks, Tintern, Tulip, Upland, and Vanbiber.

The paths are maintained, but not compulsively so: in keeping with the original City Beautiful intent, foliage is allowed to encroach but not overwhelm. Residents use the paths to get to school, to the store, to neighbors'—and, yes, in winter, to sled on, too.

THE RUBENS VASE

How on earth did this beauty survive?

There's nothing secret about the Walters. It's recognized as one of the best art museums in the country. But the museum holds many secrets, and one of them is in plain sight.

The Rubens Vase holds a prominent spot in the Early Byzantine Art section. According to the Walters's own records, the Rubens Vase was "carved in high relief from a single piece of agate . . . most likely created in an imperial workshop for a Byzantine emperor." It eventually wound up in France, "probably carried off as treasure after the sack of Constantinople in 1204." A series of notable collectors came to possess it, including King Charles V of France. But the vase takes its name from its association with the great Flemish painter Peter Paul Rubens (1577–1640). After that, from The Walters's records, this note: "The subsequent fate of the vase before the 19th century [when Henry Walters bought it] is obscure."

While working on my 2008 book, Shipwrecked!, I researched the Dutch trading vessel Batavia, which impaled itself on the reefs of the coral islands 50 miles off the coast of modern-day Australia in 1629. While the captain rowed to Indonesia to get help, an apothecary named Jeronimus Cornelisz formed a gang that took over the island, plundered the Batavia's bounty, and instituted a murderous and dictatorial regime. Each evening,

---

PETER PAUL RUBENS VASE

WHAT: A fragile, irreplaceable object with a sporadic history

WHERE: Walters Art Museum, 600 N. Charles St., Mount Vernon

COST: Free

PRO TIP: Don't just check out the vase and scram; The Walters collection "spans more than seven millennia, from 5,000 BCE to the 21st century, and encompasses 36,000 objects."

after inflicting terror on the Batavia's survivors, the gang members selected their plunder. Among the treasures: the Rubens Vase. Rubens had given the vase to the Batavia's captain to trade with the powerful Grand Moghul of India.

By the time the captain returned with a rescue ship, three months later, 120 people had been murdered. "If there ever has been a Godless man . . . it was [Cornelisz]," wrote a clergyman whose wife and six of his children were murdered.

How the fragile and exquisite vase survived a shipwreck and subsequent rough treatment by the usurpers is something of a miracle. That it sits in its placid location at The Walters is a gift for us all.

The Batavia massacre holds the distinction as the worst single-event mass murder in Australian history.

SAILORS UNION GRACE CHURCH

What on earth is a Ship Church?

Today's Sailors Union Grace Church (formerly Sailors Union Bethel Methodist Church) in Federal Hill was built in 1873 and was originally known as the Ship Church. Why? Here's the story.

In the mid-1840s, led by Samuel Kramer, a group of locals with shipping interests purchased a wrecked ship, the *William Penn*, which was at anchor at the wharves near Light Street. They, along with sailors both local and temporarily docked at the Port of Baltimore, wanted a place to worship together. Lacking a physical building, they held services on the *William Penn* after building a large roof over the hull and outfitting the ship with two dozen windows to let in the breezes off the water. It became known, not surprisingly, as the "Ship Church," and skipper Kramer became its first minister.

SHIP CHURCH

WHAT: A church with a unique historical association

WHERE: 454 E. Cross St., Federal Hill

COST: Free

PRO TIP: Less than a half mile to the west is the wonderful Cross Street Market. Originally built in 1846, the market had a makeover in 2019 that saw the restoration of the entrances on Charles and Light Streets to resemble their 1950s designs.

Conveniently, the now-departed Smokey's Bar, which catered to sailors of all stripes—devout or not—sat just down the block from the original church, at the corner of Cross and Covington.

The "Ship Church" on Cross Street in Federal Hill

Within six years, the old church on the ship was condemned. No amount of salvation could beat back the work of salt and elements. But the congregation survived, first building a church on Lee Street, then constructing a replacement structure on Cross Street in 1873.

By 1881, the church got its official name: the Sailors Union Bethel Methodist Church. A nearby historical marker notes that a "model of the *William Penn* which hangs from the ceiling of the sanctuary commemorates the church's origins."

ST. MARY'S INDUSTRIAL SCHOOL

Where did the Babe find his way to the straight and narrow?

Many Baltimoreans know the towering and impressive stone edifice at 3225 Wilkens Avenue as the old home of the Cardinal Gibbons School, which began operating in 1962 but closed down in 2010. Since that time, the school ground's athletic facilities have been used for sporting events, but the building no longer functions as a school. Nowadays, it's being incorporated into ongoing and future mixed-use plans administered by St. Agnes Hospital, across the street.

But before all this, the campus was known as St. Mary's Industrial School for Boys from its creation in 1866 until 1950. It was within this period—1902, to be exact—that St. Mary's saw the enrollment of George Herman Ruth, who would eventually become Babe Ruth. It was here where the young George learned the game of baseball from one of the school's brothers.

Learn it he did, becoming baseball's most valuable player less than 20 years later and eventually earning his place in the

---

Ruth never lost his affinity for his old school and the brothers who took the young incorrigible under their wings. When a fire ravaged a good chunk of the campus in 1919, Ruth, by then a New York Yankee, traveled to various ballparks with the school band in tow, helping to raise money for reconstruction efforts.

Where Babe Ruth went to school and learned to play baseball

record books as the greatest slugger who ever played the game.

Today, several buildings still remain from Ruth's time (indeed, predating his time there), and the baseball field, converted to turf from grass a few years ago, carries the honorific: Babe Ruth Field. It is the only such field in the country that truly deserves the name, for it is here that the lad hit his first ball, threw his first pitch, and caught his first fly ball.

THE OLD ST. MARY'S INDUSTRIAL SCHOOL

WHAT: Babe Ruth's school

WHERE: 3325 Wilkens Ave., Wilhelm Park

COST: Free

PRO TIP: Few things say Baltimore more than rowhomes with front stoops. In the 2600 block of Wilkens, to the east of Babe Ruth Field, is the longest such uninterrupted block in the city, known locally as the "Mill Hill Deck of Cards." Some believe that this may be the longest unbroken row of houses not only in Baltimore, but in the world.

SIDESHOW

Can a sideshow also be a main attraction?

In December 2019, the *Washington Post* profiled the American Visionary Art Museum (AVAM). No huge surprise there, as AVAM has been garnering raves from news outlets across the country for decades. CNN called it "one of the most fantastic museums anywhere in America." And CNBC declared AVAM's November 2020 25-year anniversary retrospective one of its "Museum exhibits worth planning a trip around in 2020." Those of us who live here and have visited many times know these plaudits to be earned. AVAM is, quite simply, a magical place.

But what isn't quite as well known to the outside world is the magic of its museum shop. Most people view museum shops as places with extraordinarily overpriced items through which to run a commercial gauntlet after being funneled through exhibits. Not Sideshow, which has one entrance situated separately from AVAM's exhibits.

Here you are free to pick up, test, check out, shake your head at, or laugh about the merchandise. Don't be surprised if you easily while away an hour here. It's as if you've stumbled

AVAM SIDESHOW

WHAT: Museum shop

WHERE: Sideshow at the American Visionary Art Museum, 800 Key Hwy., Federal Hill

COST: $9.95–$15.95 for the museum; but free to just browse Sideshow.

PRO TIP: Don't forget to catch AVAM's Kinetic Sculpture Race in the spring, "a race through Baltimore of wacky, imaginative, totally human-powered works of art, designed to travel on land, through mud, and over deep Baltimore Inner Harbor waters, constructed out of used bicycles, gears, and parts, created by a lunatic genius who tinkers around in the garage or backyard."

American Visionary Art Museum gift shop

upon your weird uncle's lifetime collection of oddities that he's stored in his massive basement. Divided into three sections—books, novelties, and original art—are inexpensive trinkets and gag gifts as well as legitimate original art that is pricey but that will be as unique a gift as the outsider art in the museum itself. You will never be disappointed here and are guaranteed a good time.

A new café opened in AVAM in 2020—Cielo Verde—and if initial reviews are any indication, it's as much a winner as everything else AVAM offers.

SIMPLY DIVINE

What does Baltimore's favorite drag queen look like when he's three stories tall?

Divine, born Harris Glenn Milstead in Baltimore, became a cult hero for his roles in many John Waters's films, memorably consuming dog feces in *Pink Flamingos* and playing the inimitable Edna Turnblad in *Hairspray*, among his other roles. He has been dubbed the "Drag Queen of the Century" by *People* magazine.

So of course it makes perfect sense for a Mount Vernon couple to have an image of Divine painted on the side of their three-story rowhouse. The image itself comes from Divine's 1984 disco single "I'm So Beautiful," and it's a lovely display—though it takes a bit of sleuthing to spot it , as large as it is, because it faces an alley.

DIVINE MURAL

WHAT: The city's, and perhaps the world's, only mural dedicated to a drag queen

WHERE: 106 E. Preston St., Midtown-Belvedere/Mount Vernon Historical District

COST: Free

PRO TIP: Milstead is buried in the Prospect Hill Park Cemetery in Towson, just north of Baltimore, in Baltimore County.

But Divine's image was almost gone before it had much of an opportunity to get comfortable. The couple living in the house on Preston Street commissioned the mural by Baltimore artist Gaia without first getting the necessary permit to alter the exterior of their home, which falls inside a historic district.

The mural is a mere six blocks from the corner of Read and Tyson Streets, where the infamous dog feces scene from Pink Flamingos was shot.

Divine at the American Visionary Art Museum

"I'm So Beautiful" indeed. Baltimore's favorite drag queen, Divine

Because the image was created over unpainted bricks, it ran afoul of historic ordinances. But—ironically—removing the paint would have constituted yet a second violation. So good old Divine is there to stay and should keep watch over Midtown-Belvedere for years to come. John Waters himself weighed in after the decision: "I think Preston Street now has the ultimate Neighborhood Watch."

Only in Baltimore.

ST. PAUL'S LUTHERAN CEMETERY

Who were Victoria and George Atzerodt?

Most folks around here are familiar with the roster of notables buried at the beautiful Greenmount Cemetery, established in 1838. Among its 65,000 interred are John Wilkes Booth; circus performer Johnny Eck, aka the King of the Freaks; eight Maryland governors; eight Baltimore mayors; Johns Hopkins; Henry Walters; Enoch Pratt; and Napoleon Bonaparte's sister-in-law, Betsy Patterson, who married Prince Jerome Bonaparte in 1805. They lived at 609 North Charles Street, in Mount Vernon.

There's also Mount Auburn Cemetery on the west side, once known as the City of the Dead for Colored People. It dates to 1872, when cemeteries were segregated, making it one of the oldest "colored" graveyards in the country. Among those buried there are Lillie May Carroll Jackson, leader of the Baltimore chapter of the NAACP for 35 years; John Henry Murphy, the founder of *The Afro-American* newspaper; and Joe Gans, the first African American boxing lightweight champion and widely considered the greatest lightweight boxer ever. And then there is the diminutive Fells Family Cemetery in Fells Point, sandwiched inconspicuously between two rowhouses.

There are, of course, plenty of other graveyards in Baltimore. But one, in Druid Hill Park, is not very well known: St. Paul's

---

George Atzerodt was hanged along with his three co-conspirators—Lewis Powell, David Herold, and Mary Surratt—in July 1865 in Washington, DC. The story is told in Robert Redford's 2010 movie, *The Conspirator.*

Hidden Druid Hill Park cemetery, with connection to Abraham Lincoln

A CEMETERY IN DRUID HILL PARK

WHAT: The gravestone of a would-be Lincoln assassination co-conspirator

WHERE: Shop Rd., Druid Hill Park

COST: Free

PRO TIP: The cemetery is today overseen and cared for by the Martini Lutheran Church on West Henrietta Street in Sharp-Leadenhall. The church offers for sale a 24-page booklet, *A Complete History of the Cemetery Using Original Source Material Found in the Files of Martini Lutheran Church*, and proceeds go to charity.

Lutheran Cemetery (1854). Its obscurity is due in part to the fact that it was left to molder for decades before a restoration project was launched in 2011. Nowadays, its gravestones are righted, the weeds pulled, and the glorious wrought iron gates restored.

But the graveyard still holds a secret: Victoria Atzerodt and her son, George Atzerodt, are buried here. (You won't see their names on any tombstones, though. Instead, look for Gottlieb Taubert). So, who were they? George Atzerodt was one of the Lincoln assassination conspirators; his role was to kill Vice President Andrew Johnson, an act he ultimately never attempted. When George was posthumously pardoned by Johnson, Victoria obtained George's remains and arranged for them to be buried in a family plot under the name of Gottlieb Taubert, presumed to be a fictional name.

STONY RUN FIREFLIES

Where can you bask in the splendor of a free light show?

Fireflies (or, "lightning bugs," if you prefer) are freedom, and summer, and innocence, and beauty, and wonder. The list of superlatives can go on and on. There's perhaps nothing that better forces us to slow down, breathe in, take stock, and enjoy the wonders of the world around us than the sight of these electric beetles flashing on a summer night.

Those of us who grew up in areas with fireflies can perhaps take it for granted. But fireflies don't generally range past the Midwest, so many of our western friends have not had the opportunity to experience the sublimity of these amazing creatures Witnessing a night sky filled with their insistent blinking is a thing not easily forgotten.

There's a spot along Stony Run, in north-central Baltimore, that consistently yields a tremendous concentration of these

> ### FIREFLY FEST
>
> **WHAT:** A summertime light show
>
> **WHERE:** Stony Run, between W. Cold Spring Ln. and Wyndhurst Ave., Wyndhurst/Roland Park
>
> **COST:** Free
>
> **PRO TIP:** Bolton Street Synagogue graciously permits parking in its lot (follow signage as to where exactly) so people can access the trail just off West Cold Spring Lane.

Stony Run Trail runs roughly 2.5 miles from the Gilman and Friends Schools area in Roland Park through a dozen neighborhoods, incorporating parts of the Johns Hopkins University and the Wyman Dell.

Stony Run Trail

insects; the stretch of creek between West Cold Spring Lane and Wyndhurst Avenue seems to contain the perfect habitat for fireflies: access to water, tall grass, and not a lot of ambient light to ruin the show. In many places, a backyard will suffice, but if you really want to see them at their concentrated best, head here.

Now, if we humans could just figure out how fireflies manage to generate light without heat, we might have the key to reversing the most deleterious effects of climate change. Yet another reason to love those little things.

SWIMMING WITH THE FISHES

How can you swim with coral reef life downtown?

One of the great things about living in Baltimore is our proximity to so much water. Taking all its inlets and coves, Maryland actually has more coastline than California (seriously—look it up).

But if you're downtown and you want to do some spectacular snorkeling or scuba, you need to get to the ocean. You can be there in a couple of hours from the city, but mid-Atlantic snorkeling and scuba isn't quite like it is in the Caribbean. The good news is that if you're downtown, you'll find good diving if you just stay put. So what's the deal?

To be fair, this one comes with some caveats and requirements. First, here's what you'll need to do: bring roughly $200; be at least 18 years old; have scuba diving certification with the PADI® Open Water Diver course; and bring your own wetsuit, mask, snorkel, and scuba fins.

Once you've cleared those hurdles, you're eligible to dive into the tank at the National Aquarium and take your place for 30 to 45 minutes in the Atlantic coral reef exhibit—an impressive 335,000-gallon, 13-foot-deep exhibit of nearly 1,000 varieties of colorful tropical marine life,

NATIONAL AQUARIUM SCUBA DIVING

WHAT: Swimming with Atlantic coral reef life

WHERE: National Aquarium in Baltimore, 501 E. Pratt St., Downtown

COST: $195 for the tour

PRO TIP: Diving is done at the aquarium, but to book the trip, go through the Atlantic Edge Dive Center: www.atlanticedge.com.

View of the National Aquarium from atop Federal Hill

including moray eels, bonnethead sharks, and spotfin porcupinefish. Those are just some of the show-stealers. In all, there are more than 90 species of rays, sharks, and fish in the tank. Better yet, dives are limited to six people, so it's a pretty intimate experience.

The Guest Dive Tour isn't the only Tour & Experience offered; for a complete list, check out aqua.org/Visit/Tours-and-Experiences.

THURGOOD MARSHALL'S BOYHOOD HOME

Where did the country's first African American Supreme Court justice grow up?

It is, admittedly, a somewhat tortured relationship: the state of Maryland nowadays understandably embraces the towering figure that is Thurgood Marshall, the country's first African American Supreme Court justice. State officials renamed Baltimore-Washington International Airport as Baltimore/Washington International Thurgood Marshall Airport in 2005, and the University of Maryland law library is called the University of Maryland Thurgood Marshall Law Library.

The recognition, though belated, is of course deserved. There is a bit of irony here, however, as it was the University of Maryland's refusal in 1930 to accept Marshall as a student based on his race that set him on the path to fighting such injustice in the first place. Likewise, while a prominent statue of Marshall now graces the entrance to the downtown Baltimore building that houses the US District Court and Court of Appeals, considering the overt segregation in Baltimore during his childhood, Marshall understandably did not have much love for his hometown. Nevertheless, his being a native Baltimorean does mean the city can claim yet another prominent figure in the history of the nation.

Marshall became a federal judge in 1961 under appointment of John F. Kennedy and, after a stint as US solicitor general, was appointed to the Supreme Court in 1967, serving until 1991.

Where the nation's first African American Supreme Court justice grew up

CHILDHOOD HOME OF THURGOOD MARSHALL

WHAT: Historical site

WHERE: 1632 Division St., Madison Park

COST: Free

PRO TIP: Division Street is just a block and a half from Pennsylvania Avenue and thus sits within the Pennsylvania Avenue Black Arts and Entertainment District, an area rich in history.

Marshall was born here in July of 1908 and grew up at 1632 Division Street, off the once-thriving Black entertainment district on Pennsylvania Avenue. The tidy brick house where he grew up, second from the corner near the intersection of Wilson Street, today has a historical plaque.

After being denied admission to the University of Maryland Law School, he earned his degree from Howard and then returned to Baltimore to practice law. He ultimately, and successfully, sued the University of Maryland, forcing the school to admit Black students to its law program. Marshall then embarked on an extraordinary string of successes arguing before the US Supreme Court, including as part of the team that argued *Brown v. Board of Education of Topeka*.

THE 2 O'CLOCK CLUB

Where does the spirit of burlesque (try to) live on?

Let's be honest. The 400 block of East Baltimore Street—or, as it is better known, "The Block"—has seen better days. But time was, this area was famous for its respectable (enough) burlesque houses, and the epicenter was The 2 O'clock Club for one primary reason: Blaze Starr, the most famous burlesque performer of all time.

Starr made her debut at the club in 1950, and by 1968 she owned the joint. Her singular stage presence made a trip to The 2 O'clock Club a rite of passage for young men up and down the East Coast.

Her 2015 *Baltimore Sun* obituary noted that Ms. Starr was a "performer who brought to The Block a playful version of stripping that combined the flair of an entertainer and the attitude of a satirist." The obit also noted that her persona was so beloved and non-threatening that she once appeared in ads for Baltimore Gas & Electric. Even the incumbent mayor during Starr's reign had a soft spot for her, declaring: "We would go down to The 2 O'clock Club, and I would give her the key to the city. I caught a lot of hell for it but it was a good time." Indeed, Starr was adored, larger than life, and well ahead of her time, advocating for women's rights and civil rights before such things were in vogue. Among other

BYGONE BURLESQUE

WHAT: Club where Blaze Starr starred

WHERE: 414 E. Baltimore St., Downtown

COST: None to look; how much you spend inside is, of course, up to you.

PRO TIP: While some visitors are turned off by what they perceive as the seedy nature of The Block, note that a central police station is a mere 500 feet east on Baltimore Street.

The 2 O'clock Club, home of Blaze Starr,
history's most famous burlesque performer

endearing qualities, she had a soft spot for veterans, giving them free shows and in the process earning commendations from the American Legion. John Waters credited Blaze Starr with aiding in his ultimate formation as well.

Starr's affair with Louisiana Governor Earl Young was recounted in the Paul Newman movie, *Blaze*.

UNDER LEXINGTON MARKET

What lurks under Baltimore's sidewalks?

Baltimore's underground network is extensive and extraordinary. A veritable mirror city functions underneath the one we traverse every day. Sewers, subways, train tracks, rivers, gas and electric—a steaming grate is a reminder of this amazing and increasingly vulnerable subterranean world. But as a general rule, we tend to not think much about it unless its reminders force themselves upon us: a ruptured water main or subsequent sinkhole, for example.

So it's worthwhile to stay above ground and while there head to Lexington Market to grab a crab cake and a drink. Ralph Waldo Emerson called Lexington Market "the gastronomic capital of the world." It has been in continuous operation since 1782, making it the country's oldest. But don't leave so quickly. Why not head *under* the market as well?

During the 1951 construction of the adjacent parking garage, the tunnels under Lexington Market were rediscovered. They were originally installed not long after the Civil War. The conjecture is that pre-refrigeration, the tunnels were used for meat storage.

More interesting—though unconfirmed—suggestions for past usage include whiskey production during Prohibition, a gathering place for communist sympathizers, and even part

---

Included in the tours are discussions with selected vendors at the market who have been in their stalls 100 or more years.

Butcher shops at Lexington Market

BELOW GROUND AT LEXINGTON MARKET

WHAT: Tunnels housing secrets

WHERE: Lexington Market, 400 W. Lexington St., Downtown

COST: $10

PRO TIP: Baltimore Heritage provides weekend tours of the tunnels: baltimoreheritage.org/tours.

of the Underground Railroad. One wonderful anecdote has kids scraping together ice from refrigeration units and having snowball fights in July. More contemporaneously, there was even a restaurant and nightclub that functioned down there—Tubbs—which lasted all the way until 1988. Weekend tours through Baltimore Heritage shed light on all these stories, both established and conjectured.

ZORA WAS HERE

Would we know one of America's greatest writers had she not come to Baltimore?

Yuval Taylor, in his 2019 book, *Zora and Langston: A Story of Friendship and Betrayal*, includes the astonishing fact that "[Hurston's] 1937 *Their Eyes Were Watching God* remains the single most widely read book ever written by an African American. It outsells even *Invisible Man, I Know Why the Caged Bird Sings, The Color Purple, Raisin in the Sun, Narrative of the Life of Frederick Douglass*, and *The Autobiography of Malcolm X*."

Hurston is often referred to as one of the great "African American female" writers, and this reduction does her a disservice. Nowadays, we know Hurston as one of America's greatest writers, no matter the category. Hurston's contributions to the literary landscape of America, as a novelist, playwright, and folklorist, are almost unparalleled. She became one of the central figures of the Harlem Renaissance and produced numerous works, the most recent published in 2018, almost 60 years after her death.

MORGAN STATE UNIVERSITY

WHAT: Where Zora Neale Hurston attended

WHERE: Morgan State University, E. Cold Spring Ln., Hillen

COST: Free

PRO TIP: It is hard to actually "see" much of Hurston at today's Morgan, so if you are looking for a more tangible literary landmark, check out the Continental Trust Building, 201 East Baltimore Street, downtown. It was here where the writer Dashiell Hammett (*The Maltese Falcon, The Thin Man*) worked for many years for the Pinkerton Detective Agency, no doubt storing up material for his later work.

Morgan State, once Morgan Academy, where Zora Neale Hurston studied

But her early years were challenging ones, and formal education wasn't in the cards for Ms. Hurston. Into her 20s, she faced a life of obscurity. But then she arrived in Baltimore in 1916, working as a maid for a traveling music troupe. By all accounts, this is the life she would have continued to live had an emergency appendectomy not landed her at Maryland General Hospital.

The troupe traveled on, and Zora stayed in the city with her sister. Here, she enrolled at Morgan Academy, which was at the time a high school branch of today's Morgan State University. She lied about her age to get in and was a good decade older than many of her classmates. But she got that schooling, completing her graduation requirements two years later, and a life of letters opened up to her. There would be no turning back.

Cool addendum: two decades after Hurston left, she received an honorary doctorate from what was then called Morgan State College.

The Morgan State University choir is world-renowned, literally celebrated all across the globe. Hearing them sing is a life-altering experience. To check them out: www.msuchoir.org

SOURCES

The *Afro* and the Upton
https://www.afro.com/about-us
https://baltimoreheritage.org/issue/upton-mansion
https://www.baltimoresun.com/business/real-estate/bs-bz-afro-returns-to-west-baltimore-upton-mansion-20200226-cslog5cnvfdypo36z4sfzx63be-story.html

Al Capone's Cherry Trees
https://www.baltimoresun.com/ph-ms-union-memorial-0329-20120326-story.html
https://historycollection.co/al-capone-hospital-treated-debilitating-syphilis/3
http://welcometobaltimorehon.com/al-capones-cherry-tree

Arabber Stables
https://www.baltimoresun.com/entertainment/arts/bs-fe-lewis-arabbers-20190227-story.html
https://www.baltimoresun.com/opinion/op-ed/bs-ed-op-0417-arabbers-20180416-story.html

The Other Arboretum
http://www.miniarboretum.org

Archaeological Museum
http://archaeologicalmuseum.jhu.edu

Babe's Baptism
https://cruxnow.com/faith/2016/02/for-babe-ruth-catholicism-was-a-lifelong-pursuit
https://www.baltimoresun.com/maryland/bs-md-ci-st-peter-church-20120127-story.html

Baltimore, France
https://artbma.org/exhibitions/cone-collection
https://www.smithsonianmag.com/smart-news/baltimore-museum-home-largest-matisse-collection-will-open-center-dedicated-artist-180972741

Baltimore Greenway Trails Network
https://www.railstotrails.org/our-work/trailnation/baltimore-greenway-trails-coalition
https://www.bikemore.net/greenwaytrailsnetwork

Totally Bazaar
https://www.bazaarbaltimore.com
https://en.wikipedia.org/wiki/American_Dime_Museum

Bennett Blazers
https://bennettblazers.org/wheelchair-basketball
https://www.baltimoresun.com/sports/bs-md-bennett-blazers-20190401-story.html

Billie Holiday Alley
https://www.facebook.com/BaltimoreBillieHolidayProject

BMA at Lexington Market
https://artbma.org/visit/outpost.html
https://lexingtonmarket.com/vendor/bma-lexington-market
https://www.baltimoresun.com/entertainment/arts/bs-fe-bma-lexingtonmarket-20190625-story.html

Bolton Hill Blue Plaques
https://baltimoreheritage.org/project/bolton-hill-blue-plaques
https://sites.google.com/view/boltonhill-org/home

The Book Thing
https://bookthing.org
https://www.osibaltimore.org/2017/07/osi-fellows-mural-arts-programs-with-bopas-artwork-to-hold-unveiling/

BUS Stop—Literally and Figuratively
https://slate.com/human-interest/2014/08/bus-by-spanish-artist-collective-mmmm-is-the-worlds-most-obvious-bus-stop-design-photos.html
https://creativealliance.org/2014-07/bus-sculpture-unveiling

Chesapeake & Allegheny Steam Preservation Society
http://calslivesteam.org

Baltimore's China (er, Ethiopia) Town
https://www.baltimoresun.com/food-drink/bs-fe-charm-city-night-market-20180919-story.html
https://charmcitynightmarket.com
https://www.facebook.com/thechinatowncollective
https://thechinatowncollective.wedid.it

Carrollton Viaduct
https://en.wikipedia.org/wiki/Carrollton_Viaduct
https://bridgehunter.com/md/baltimore-city/carrollton
https://explore.baltimoreheritage.org/items/show/76
https://www.asce.org/project/carrollton-viaduct

The Oldest Columbus
https://www.baltimoresun.com/maryland/baltimore-city/bs-md-ci-pugh-columbus-20171009-story.html
https://en.wikipedia.org/wiki/Columbus_Obelisk

Confederate Executions
http://www.federalhillonline.com/tourstop02.htm

Costume Shop
https://www.baltimoremagazine.com/2018/3/12/on-with-the-show-a-t-jones-sons-costume-shop-turns-150
https://baltimoreheritage.org/legacy-business-a-t-jones-sons

The Country's First Strip Mall
https://mht.maryland.gov/nr/NRDetail.aspx?NRID=263
https://www.livingplaces.com/MD/Independent_Cities/City_of_Baltimore/Roland_Park_Historic_District.html

Curtis Creek Ship Graveyard
https://www.findyourchesapeake.com/trip-ideas/article/paddling-the-curtis-creek-ship-graveyard
https://www.atlasobscura.com/places/curtis-creek-ship-graveyard
https://www.baltimoresun.com/news/bs-xpm-1995-10-14-1995287014-story.html

Dandelion, Don't Tell No Lies . . .
https://fineartamerica.com/profiles/david-tonnesen
https://www.baltimoresun.com/arcio/gallery-sitemap/?from=1500

Dickeyville
https://dickeyville.org/about-dv/village-history
https://mht.maryland.gov/nr/NRDetail.aspx?NRID=93

The Diner from *Diner*
https://www.baltimoresun.com/food-drink/bal-hollywood-diner-in-maryland-20120220-story.html
http://welcometobaltimorehon.com/the-hollywood-diner

Douglass Terrace
https://baltimore.org/article/walk-frederick-douglass-footsteps
https://en.wikipedia.org/wiki/Douglass_Place

Dragon Boat Challenge
https://www.baltimoredragonboatclub.com
https://en.wikipedia.org/wiki/Dragon_boat

Druid* and *Green Man
https://www.baltimoresun.com/maryland/bs-md-tiki-men-in-druid-hill-park-20121220-story.html
https://baltimorefishbowl.com/stories/the-amazing-tree-stump-carvings-of-druid-hill-park

Edgar Allan Poe's Last Moments
https://www.smithsonianmag.com/history/still-mysterious-death-edgar-allan-poe-180952936
https://www.history.com/news/how-did-edgar-allan-poe-die
https://www.baltimoresun.com/news/bs-xpm-1994-10-02-1994275208-story.html
https://www.mdhs.org/underbelly/2015/10/22/here-at-last-he-is-happy-the-death-and-burial-of-edgar-allan-poe

Elephants in Druid Hill
https://www.marylandzoo.org/news-and-updates/2014/06/new-elephant-sculptures-outside-zoo

Elvis Has Left the Building . . .
https://creativealliance.org/events/2019/elviss-birthday-fightclub
https://www.baltimoresun.com/food-drink/bs-ae-elvis-fight-club-20130110-story.html

Equilibrium
https://www.baltimoresun.com/entertainment/arts/bs-fe-sherald-mural-20180810-story.html
https://baltimorefishbowl.com/stories/amy-sheralds-next-big-unveiling-will-be-a-mural-in-station-north
http://www.promotionandarts.org/transformative-art-prize-mural-dedication-amy-sherald

Factory of Champions
https://www.teamunify.com/Home.jsp?team=msnbac
http://www.mbrook.com
https://www.teamusa.org/para-swimming/athletes/Jessica-Long
https://en.wikipedia.org/wiki/Michael_Phelps

Flag House (No, Not That One)

http://www.baltimoreinabox.com

Float Like a Butterfly, Sting Like a Bee

https://www.facebook.com/pages/Upton-Boxing-Center/127855123951098

https://bcrp.baltimorecity.gov/upton-boxing-center

https://www.baltimoresun.com/sports/bs-sp-gervonta-davis-boxing-scene-20190727-qrsntpp5zzfcxcddxe3wxrqkju-story.html

https://www.nytimes.com/2017/02/24/sports/gervonta-davis-baltimore.html

Frank Zappa's Head

https://www.theguardian.com/music/2008/may/09/news

https://www.summitdaily.com/news/bust-of-frank-zappa-to-be-erected-in-hometown-of-baltimore

https://www.baltimoresun.com/bs-mtblog-2009-12-frank_zappa_statue_to_go_near-story.html

Free Concerts

hub.jhu.edu/events/?locations=peabody-institute

Gas Lighting (Two Words, Not One)

https://aoghs.org/technology/manufactured-gas

https://americangaslamp.com/recognizing-first-gas-street-lamp-america

https://www.thepealecenter.org/gas-light-at-the-peale

https://www.baltimoresun.com/features/retro-baltimore/bs-fe-retro-gas-lighters-20170824-story.html

Graffiti Alley

https://www.baltimoresun.com/baltimores-best/bal-best-of-baltimore-best-kept-secret-story.html

http://graffitiwarehouse.com

https://hiddenbaltimore.wordpress.com/2012/11/13/baltimores-graffiti-alley

Great Baltimore Oyster Partnership

https://www.waterfrontpartnership.org/healthy-harbor/oyster-partnership

https://www.cbf.org/how-we-save-the-bay/programs-initiatives/maryland/oyster-restoration/oyster-gardening/oyster-gardening-in-the-inner-harbor.html

https://baltimore.cbslocal.com/2019/09/26/great-baltimore-oyster-partnerships-oyster-gardening-volunteer-workshop

Hansa Haus

https://www.explorebaltimore.org/places/hansa-haus

https://baltimoreheritage.org/bbotw-hansa-haus

https://www.baltimoresun.com/news/bs-xpm-2000-10-14-0010140288-story.html

https://www.baltimoresun.com/news/bs-xpm-2001-10-28-0110270147-story.html

Hebrew Orphan Asylum

https://baltimorefishbowl.com/stories/17-million-renovation-begins-on-former-hebrew-orphan-asylum

https://explore.baltimoreheritage.org/items/show/111

https://www.baltimoresun.com/maryland/baltimore-city/bs-md-ci-kelly-column-orphanage-20190502-story.html

https://www.baltimoresun.com/maryland/baltimore-city/bs-md-ci-kelly-column-orphan-20181218-story.html

https://www.jmoreliving.com/2018/12/20/hebrew-orphan-asylum-to-be-repurposed-as-health-care-facility

House of Pain
https://www.dental.umaryland.edu/museum

https://www.umaryland.edu/about-umb/davidge-hall

https://medicalalumni.org/history-of-davidge-hall

Irish Railroad Workers Museum
http://www.irishshrine.org

Joseph Kavanagh Co., Practical Coppersmiths
https://www.baltimoremagazine.com/section/historypolitics/joseph-kavanagh-company-coppersmithing-bootlegging-prohibition

http://josephkavanaghco.com/about.html

Kite Celebration
https://www.creativealliance.org/events/2020/2nd-big-baltimore-kite-fest

https://baltimore.org/events/big-baltimore-kite-fest

G. Krug & Son
https://gkrugandson.com

https://explore.baltimoreheritage.org/items/show/161

London Coffee House
https://www.baltimoresun.com/news/bs-xpm-2000-05-11-0005110069-story.html

http://www.baltimoremd.com/fellstour/4.html

https://www.bizjournals.com/baltimore/stories/2000/03/27/story5.html

Lovely Lane United Methodist Church
http://www.lovelylane.net

https://explore.baltimoreheritage.org/items/show/37

http://lovelylanemuseum.org/index.html

Maryland School for the Blind
https://www.marylandschoolfortheblind.org

https://www.marylandschoolfortheblind.org/programs-services/student-services/athletics

https://www.baltimoresun.com/sports/high-school/bs-sp-va-msb-soccer-0925-20190924-xzuawreys5ayniha3pkclwsfda-story.html

https://www.msn.com/en-us/video/be-prepared/maryland-school-for-the-blind-hosted-first-competitive-youth-blind-soccer-match-in-the-us/vp-AAHNsHw

Maryland Science Center Observatory
https://www.mdsci.org/explore/science-encounters/observatory

https://www.mdsci.org/event/friday-night-stargazing

His Master's Voice, Writ Large
https://www.ohmidog.com/2009/12/03/a-tale-of-two-cities-and-two-nippers/

http://www.mdhs.org/plan-visit/faq

https://en.wikipedia.org/wiki/His_Master%27s_Voice

The McKim Center / Quaker Friends Meeting House
https://www.mckimcenter.org

https://explore.baltimoreheritage.org/items/show/203

Memorial Stadium
https://en.wikipedia.org/wiki/Memorial_Stadium_(Baltimore)

https://www.baltimoresun.com/business/bs-bz-senior-housing-for-memorial-stadium-site-20190816-5ok32yig5vdqra4e6tzhuxeu3y-story.html

Miss Carter's Kitchen
https://www.baltimoresun.com/food-drink/bs-md-miss-carters-kitchen-lamar-jackson-20200111-v6zlq65p65eqjhqwh7fvrs6gzu-story.html

"The Most Dangerous of All Allied Spies"
https://www.baltimoresun.com/maryland/baltimore-county/bs-md-co-virginia-hall-marker-20180404-story.html

https://www.history.com/news/female-allied-spy-world-war-2-wooden-leg

https://allthatsinteresting.com/virginia-hall

https://www.baltimoresun.com/features/retro-baltimore/bs-md-kelly-virginia-hall-20200111-6qeyyfkygrazfurs7och6v6ki-story.html

The Name Remains the Same . . .
http://www.alexbrownbranches.com/baltimore/history.asp

https://planning.baltimorecity.gov/sites/default/files/History%20of%20Baltimore.pdf

Naturalization
https://www.mdd.uscourts.gov/naturalization-ceremonies

Nut and Bolt
https://www.baltimorearts.org/public-art-field-trip-nut-and-bolt

https://www.baltimorecityschools.org/schools/66

Nutshell Studies of Unexplained Death
https://americanart.si.edu/exhibitions/nutshells

http://www.deathindiorama.com

https://www.wypr.org/post/mother-forensic-science

Old St. Paul's
https://stpaulsbaltimore.org

https://www.baltimoresun.com/maryland/baltimore-city/bs-md-ci-st-pauls-church-anniversary-20170914-story.html

https://explore.baltimoreheritage.org/items/show/284

Open Doors
https://www.doorsopenbaltimore.org

Orpheus Scott Key
https://explore.baltimoreheritage.org/items/show/570

https://www.nps.gov/fomc/learn/historyculture/upload/Orpheus2_InD.pdf

https://retrobaltimore.tumblr.com/post/126622782319/orpheus-walking-at-fort-mchenry

The Ottobar
https://www.rollingstone.com/music/music-lists/10-best-live-music-venues-in-america-767070/ottobar-baltimore-767244

https://baltimorefishbowl.com/stories/rolling-stone-names-ottobar-one-of-the-10-best-live-music-venues-in-america

https://www.baltimoresun.com/features/baltimore-insider/bs-fe-rolling-stone-names-ottobar-10-best-live-music-venue-20181214-story.html

http://www.theottobar.com

Ouija Board 7-11

https://www.museumoftalkingboards.com/history.html

http://www.thingsmagazine.net/morbid-curiosity

https://www.baltimoresun.com/maryland/baltimore-city/bs-md-ci-kelly-column-ouija-20150417-column.html

Excuse My Dust

https://dorothyparker.com/dorothy-parker-haunts/baltimore-naacp

https://www.npr.org/2012/06/07/154148811/how-dorothy-parker-came-to-rest-in-baltimore

Pool No. 2

http://mencken.org/text/txt001/mencken.h-l.1948.tennis-order.htm

https://explore.baltimoreheritage.org/items/show/500

https://grahamprojects.com/2014/01/memorial-pool

Psychedelic, Man

http://lightvwbus.com/dr-bob-hieronimus

https://www.baltimoremagazine.com/2010/6/6/the-hieronimus-code

Pushpin Bus Shelter

https://www.baltimoresun.com/features/baltimore-insider/bal-highlands-pushpin-bus-stop-lets-everyone-know-we-re-here-20151112-story.html

https://www.baltimorebrew.com/2015/11/08/neighborhoods-pushpin-sculpture-says-hey-city-pay-attention-to-us

Pyramids on the Patapsco

http://jimsanborn.net

https://explore.baltimoreheritage.org/items/show/668

Roland Park Paths

rolandpark.org/wp-content/uploads/2016/05/RPFootpaths.pdf

The Rubens Vase

https://art.thewalters.org/detail/10284/the-rubens-vase

Sailors Union Grace Church

http://sailorsunionchurch.org

http://www.federalhillonline.com/tourstop04.htm

St. Mary's Industrial School

http://www.historyshomes.com/detail.cfm?id=800

https://en.wikipedia.org/wiki/Cardinal_Gibbons_School_(Baltimore,_Maryland)

https://entertainment.howstuffworks.com/babe-ruth2.htm

https://deadballbaseball.com/?p=1678

Sideshow

http://www.sideshowbaltimore.com

Simply Divine

https://www.baltimoresun.com/features/baltimore-insider/bs-fe-divine-mural-approved-20181114-story.html

https://www.baltimoresun.com/features/baltimore-insider/bs-fe-gaia-divine-mural-20181024-story.html

https://www.bizjournals.com/baltimore/news/2018/11/13/mural-of-local-film-legend-divine-aint-going.html

St. Paul's Lutheran Cemetery

https://www.germanmarylanders.org/cemeteries/st-paul-s-druid-hill

https://carolshouse.com/cemeteryrecords/stpaul

https://martinilutheran.org/2013/07/the-care-of-st-pauls-cemetery-in-druid-hill-park

https://www.baltimoresun.com/maryland/bs-xpm-2011-07-08-bs-md-backstory-cemetery-20110708-story.html

https://boothiebarn.com/2012/08/25/finding-george-atzerodt

Stony Run Fireflies

http://stonyrun.org/what-we-do/walking-path

Swimming with the Fishes

aqua.org/Visit/Tours-and-Experiences

www.atlanticedge.com

Thurgood Marshall's Boyhood Home

https://www.explorebaltimore.org/places/thurgood-marshalls-childhood-home

https://www.baltimoresun.com/features/retro-baltimore/bs-md-ci-retro-thurgood-marshalls-division-street-20171018-story.html

The 2 O'Clock Club

https://www.baltimoresun.com/obituaries/bal-notable-quotes-about-blaze-starr-20150616-photogallery.html

https://www.baltimoresun.com/citypaper/bcpnews-after-making-the-2-o-clock-club-world-famous-blaze-starr-shook-up-louisiana-politics-20150616-story.html

https://www.baltimoresun.com/obituaries/bs-md-ob-blaze-starr-20150615-story.html

Under Lexington Market

https://www.baltimoresun.com/maryland/baltimore-city/bs-md-lexington-market-catacombs-20190308-story.html

http://darkroom.baltimoresun.com/2016/07/exploring-lexington-markets-underground-vaults/#1

https://lexingtonmarket.com/event/baltimore-heritage-tour-of-lexington-market-catacombs-100-year-vendors-and-history-at-lexington-market

Zora Was Here

http://baltimoreauthors.ubalt.edu/writers/zorahurston.htm

https://www.zoranealehurston.com/about

https://www.baltimoresun.com/news/bs-xpm-2005-03-02-0503020242-story.html

INDEX